The Spirituality of Nonviolent Communication
A Course in Living Compassion

The Spirituality of Nonviolent Communication

A Course in Living Compassion

Robert Gonzales

With Filipa Hope, Simone Anliker, and Lynd Morris

Book design and layout by Simone Anliker
Cover art by Wallace Brazzeal
Interior graphic art by Herman Veluwenkamp

Independently published by Ruth Joy
(ISBN: 979-8-8477094-2-2)

Also by Robert Gonzales
Reflections on Living Compassion:
Awakening Our Passion and Living in Compassion
(ISBN: 978-0-9836635-5-3)

The Center for Living Compassion
living-compassion.org

To Robert

CONTENTS

INTRODUCTION

This book is based on the online program "The Spirituality of Nonviolent Communication: A Course in Living Compassion". It was offered from October to December 2020 by international Nonviolent Communication (NVC) teacher and Living Compassion developer Robert Gonzales. After publishing *Reflections on Living Compassion: Awakening Our Passion and Living in Compassion*[1] in 2015, Robert decided to create a series of books sharing his life work of Living Compassion. This online course—intended for those who'd already participated in five or more days of NVC training—was to become the basis for the first book in that series. Sadly, Robert passed away before he was able to make these publications a reality. However, some dedicated friends and colleagues have taken up this project to realize Robert's vision for sharing his work and contributing to more people's lives through Living Compassion.

This book is about the way Robert conceptualized living into the principles of NVC within us and between us. He called this "A two-fold spiritual life practice for living compassion" and he described it as the spiritual basis of Nonviolent Communication. When promoting this program, Robert said, "This material is an invitation to develop a foundational consciousness. To fully empower our place in life, we must first cultivate and strengthen our center from which we engage with life. When we act from our center, fueled by love, we start to harness a force that is beyond what we've known is possible."

In memory of Robert's life and his outstanding contributions to the world, and in loving service to making his teachings available for all, we present you with *The Spirituality of Nonviolent Communication: A Course in Living Compassion*. We have attempted to keep as close to Robert's actual words as possible to convey his presence to you. We trust this will be as profoundly meaningful a journey with Robert for you as it has been, and is, for us.

Filipa Hope (New Zealand), Simone Anliker (Switzerland), and Lynd Morris (United States)
The Publication Team

FOREWORD

As long as I have known Robert, he has been passionate about contributing to others. Through his courses and work with countless individuals, he has guided transformation, healing, and awakening within others. I have been privileged to be at Robert's side throughout his last 28 years. I have watched him develop the work that he grew into Living Compassion.

Robert has always been guided by an inner knowing and deeper wisdom. He had a profound spiritual experience as a child that formed and informed his life. The insights he has shared throughout his life always came from his own experiences. He would spend long periods of time in reflection, connecting inwardly to what only he could describe, and what fueled his life and teachings.

Robert lived what he taught. He embodied Living Compassion. He lived fully present to all of his experiences. Watching him accept and embrace even that which was emotionally uncomfortable or painful was an example of and inspiration for what is possible. Even in the midst of the most challenging experiences, I saw his ability to be authentic, vulnerable, and honest with himself as a deep commitment to self-love and care. Robert knew the power of being fully present to life. His practice of this inspired others and informed his work.

I am deeply grateful to Simone, Filipa, and Lynd for bringing Robert's own words into book form to be available to greater numbers of people. The information and processes offered here carry deeper truths that welcome us to return to them over time. I invite you to come back to this book periodically. In revisiting Robert's insights, I believe understanding and experiences deepen, and the connection to our authentic selves strengthens, making our lives richer and more fulfilling. I have seen how the information presented here has healed and transformed lives. It has mine.

May this book guide you to the beauty of your own heart.

Ruth Joy, wife of Robert Gonzales

Chapter 1

The Divine is a mystery. It is unknowable and beyond qualities. It has no boundaries. It is infinite beyond any kind of conception. It is absolute in every moment, thing, and element of existence. It is everything and not any one thing. There is a no-thing-ness to this mystery. It is formless and imbued in every moment of existence and every form of being. Being is protruding from infinity as all things, from apparent nothing, blooming into glorious everything.

Sometimes this mystery is called "emptiness." Sometimes it is called "all that is." Sometimes it is called "Reality" or "God" or "the Divine." Whatever it is called, it is the very essence and fabric of existence, manifesting in every molecule

1

and particle, greater and beyond every form of its manifestation. So close, it is closer than close. So obvious, it is hidden from most, except those who have received the grace of recognition.

Where this mystery—infinite, eternal, beyond all qualities and yet in every fiber of being—meets manifest life in its most pure form, there is exquisite, ineffable beauty, compassion, and peace.

For most of us, this awe, alive presence is obscured. Those who are graced or blessed feel it as a yearning. Those who are vulnerable to the great power of this mystery have been blessed with its presence in the mystery of their living. They live in awe, joy, freedom, love, and peace. Those who have had the courage to utterly surrender with eyes wide open to the ocean of life, the power of mystery, have no self. They experience only the existence of the body-mind as an instrument of the music that this mystery plays.

These words came to me several years ago. They express what, for me, is most meaningful and essential in the word "spirituality," what the construct of spirituality points to. This book is about living in the heart of spirituality, living in freedom and in fullness. It is a book about a human spirituality that is lived inwardly, internally, and in relationships in everyday life.

The notion of spirituality is rooted in the premise that there is a spiritual dimension to our existence that manifests subjectively and intersubjectively, within and between. There is an "I" and a "we" to living, and it is the integration and embodiment of these two dimensions of life that are the focus of this book.

On a very practical level, this means bringing the notion of "the fullness of life" into our everyday life. It's not only practical but also enriching to enhance and embody these dimensions of life, as we exist individually and in the space of our relationships.

One of the ways to approach the meaning of spirituality is that it is that which is essential in life, that which touches the spirit of what a human being is. It has nothing to do with belief systems, dogma, or religion. The meaning I assign to the word "spirituality" is not contained by those conceptual systems. It is something that is universal.

The notion of spirituality in the context of Nonviolent Communication (NVC) is that we bring our deep individuality, our deep identity, into interbeing. To do this requires a necessary set of consciousness and skills and capacities. One without the other is not complete. For me, the interior, individual, subjective spirituality is not complete unless I include the intersubjective, the life that exists between us in the relational spaces.

Qualities such as compassion, honesty, and integrity are manifestations or functions of living our being in relationship. This dimension can be called "Divine." Spirituality of this sort is available to us at every moment. Whenever there is kindness in life; whenever there's understanding; whenever there is compassion; whenever there is deep, equal mattering; the Divine is present because these are the qualities of the Divine. There are many transformational processes and pointers that can support us in embodying these qualities.

NVC and Spirituality

How does this notion of spirituality relate to the practice and process of Nonviolent Communication?

For me, the most important aspect of NVC is the concept of universal human needs. Needs are the heart of the NVC process. The consciousness of needs is the beginning of the spiritual dimension in NVC. Needs are those qualities or values that are universal. I remember Marshall Rosenberg—the founder of Nonviolent Communication—saying, "Needs are the energy of life reaching for life." We all have access to this life energy within us that is always reaching for life. It emerges or emanates from our true self, our very essence. In this sense, I see spirituality as our relationship to life force. And I see "life force" as the energy that emerges or emanates from our true being as our human needs.

Those who have studied spirituality through the wisdom traditions are familiar with the concept of the essential being. The notion of the true self runs throughout the spiritual traditions. The ultimate goal of these traditions is an awakening, self-realization, or enlightenment, which transforms our identity from a separate self to wholeness. Our true nature as human beings is that we are loving, compassionate, and innately free.

A spirituality within is the interior, embodied consciousness. NVC invites us to live our spirituality as an embodied experience. When I can truly connect to the energy of needs, I experience this as something I feel in my whole body, including neurologically and cellularly, and it nourishes my body.

The way we can feel and access the true self—the spiritual core of our being—is through these qualities of needs One of the many ways to experience the qualities of our being more directly is through the longings of our heart. This is accessible to everyone. Our longings can take many different forms, and they are all felt in and through the heart.

We long for understanding. We long for respect and dignity. We long for honesty and authenticity. We long for love and support. When we get in touch with the longings of our heart, we can access our core values in life. Something that is of deep value is an aspect of my true self.

One of the strengths and benefits of NVC is that it identifies many specific and concretely available qualities that we call universal human needs. These needs are these longings that unfold from the core of our being. The spirituality of NVC is rooted in our needs because they connect us to our essence. Life force emanates from our essence; it moves in and through us; and it manifests and expresses through our longings, through our needs, and through what we value.

One description of needs that I enjoy is: *They are the holes in heaven through which God's light shines.* This is how I have experienced and made sense of the spirituality of Nonviolent Communication through the heart of our universal human needs.

Needs to Essence

There is a process I call "unfolding." If something is enfolded, it is covered up, not obvious, or readily available. However, unfolding reveals more and more of what is there. I'd like to elaborate on this using a diagram I created, "The Unfolding of Essence".

The Unfolding of Essence

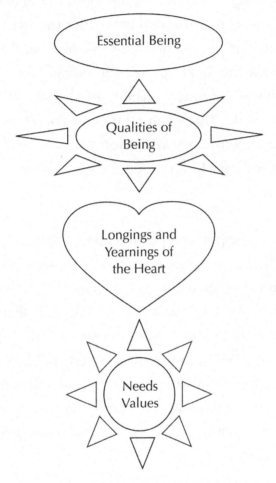

There is a basic life current or impulse resonating in and through us as a yearning of the heart, this current and yearning manifest as human needs.

This diagram demonstrates this process of "unfolding." The oval at the top of the diagram represents our essential being: our essence, our spirit, our true nature. Our essence unfolds or reveals the qualities of our being. They are inherent to the self. They are already present and whole. These natural qualities of our being reveal themselves as the longings of our heart and we refer to these longings as our needs or values.

One of the primary qualities I see as natural is the quality of love. We are naturally loving; it is our nature. We are naturally compassionate; it is our nature. Another quality of our nature is that we are absolutely free, unbounded, and unperturbed by any kind of limitation. There are a number of other qualities that are inherent to our essential being. We are not always able to connect to these qualities, and that is one of life's challenges.

There are many words that describe the core of who we are: our essence, our essential self, and our true self. This core is where all the qualities of our true self—such as innocence, creativity, aliveness, and love—reside. Whenever we are in touch with ourselves, we experience those qualities as felt, embodied energies that are unmistakably who we are. This is the part of ourselves that we want to experience in fullness. This is what we yearn for in ourselves and in our relationships. When we contact another person authentically and we experience a real connection of mutual caring, understanding, seeing, and being seen—this is the part of us that we are coming from, and it is what we are contacting in the other person.

The heart shape at the center of the diagram represents the longings of the heart, the qualities that we yearn for. If we long for support in relationships, this felt sense is already alive in our heart. I use the words "longing" and "yearning" to describe the vibration of my being. It is the vibration of the Divine in me. It is through our yearnings that most of us can more directly contact or have access to the qualities of our heart.

If I feel a longing for love or for belonging or to be seen, these tell me that my being is communicating to me through my heart. It is an energy that awakens me to what matters to me.

Our longings and yearnings of the heart unfold as our needs and values, represented in the circle at the bottom of the diagram. This is the life current moving through us as the specificity of how our longings manifest in our lives and relationships. As we've identified in the practice of Nonviolent Communication, they manifest through our needs and values.

The categories in the diagram are not strictly divided but, for me, they live as delicate distinctions. It's not the words that are important. What is important is the space within that I am experiencing and living.

The Doorway to Spirit

One of the important elements of living through and from ourselves and from our needs is that this is something that is felt. So, when we get in touch with the quality of a value or a need or longing, this is something we experience in and through our body. It is an energetic quality. When the need or longing is felt in this way, it is experienced in a much fuller way. When we are in the flow of life, we experience needs as life force.

Experiencing needs is the doorway to accessing spirituality in life and sharing our being in relationships. They are an aspect or an expression of the Divine as it lives in us. Needs arise from life. They express the requisites necessary to fulfill and nurture life itself. We experience the energy or the beauty of a need when we are in contact with the qualities of its energy. When we touch our needs, we feel their energy and experience their fullness. This opens the doorway to something more fundamental, more core.

The notion of needs being the doorway to spirit is central to the spirituality of NVC. My intention is to live in this energy of the beauty in needs as much as I can. When I am living in this energy, I am in the flow of life; whether the need is met or unmet does not affect its energy. I may mourn an unmet need, but it is the beauty of the need I mourn, not the loss of this or that outcome in life. To relate to our needs this way is transformational—for ourselves and our relationships—because healing takes place as a natural unfolding when embodying the fullness of life in the energy of our needs.

The Energies of Longing and Lack

Often, people use the word "longing" and what they mean is "seeking." There is an important distinction between longing and seeking. Longing resides in the heart as a quality that is already present. I am *already* whole as a being. I am not lacking anything. Seeking implies a lack, that I'm not experiencing something that I want to experience. For example, if I don't experience being seen or understood or if there is another unfulfilled need, I might relate to it as lacking the need rather than valuing the need. It is this experience of lack that gives rise to seeking. Seeking is a function of the mind projecting into the future. It is outcome-oriented.

One of the reasons this orientation can be limiting is that when I am expressing my need from the energy of lack or deficiency (whether spoken or not), I am communicating the energy and consciousness that something is wrong, that I'm missing something. This usually means I am attached to an outcome in some way. An orientation of lack also makes it difficult to connect with the other person's needs and requests. A verbal or energetic attachment to an outcome is communicated to the other person with the energy of "I have to have it" and a sense of urgency that comes across as a demand, even if the words are perfectly expressed according to the NVC model. As a result, when I am coming from an orientation of lack, it's almost inevitable

15

that whatever I am expressing communicates a degree of what I call "suffering."

The words "yearning" and "longing" are vibrations of the heart. Let me give you an example: How do I know that I enjoy intimacy and love? Certainly, I enjoy those qualities in real life, in the relationship spaces. But I also know and experience that these qualities are already within me: the quality of love, the quality of intimacy, the quality of beauty. It is the beauty within me that recognizes the beauty outside. It's the love that is already in me that recognizes the love in the relational space. When I touch that internal quality of love, it becomes an energy, a living impulse, that moves me toward love in my relationships. It's as though the heart is the organ of my consciousness. I want to embody my heart consciousness.

Another example of a need in relationship is the quality of belonging. If I am connecting with that energy, what I am in touch with is a space where not only I exist, but we all exist as a group. This means that when I enter into my heart, you are there, too. There is a quality of belonging in that space in which you and I already are. This may not necessarily be manifest in life, but it is manifest in that place where we exist together already. This is the living reality I get in touch with, that shows up as the longing for something beautiful.

If I am experiencing something missing, it's because of my trauma and my conditioning that orient me towards lack. My orientation changes when I'm experiencing something painful, and that pain points me to what matters to me, towards what I value.

If I am approaching another person from an orientation of lack—maybe a part of me is experiencing judgment or demand, or I want life "different than the way it is"—then I know this part of me is calling for compassion. I need to be heard more deeply about that pain so I can touch into the beauty that is underlying the need. I don't want to judge myself for experiencing lack or to tell myself that somehow lack is wrong. If I'm in this energy of lack, it means I'm in a kind of suffering pain.

When I feel a longing, on some level and to some degree, there is an experience of lack. But the part of me that recognizes the energy of lack is the longing in me. It is the longing of the dream in me that is so beautiful. It vibrates in my heart in relationship to what is in my life. Longing is aware. Longing is reminding me, it is calling to me, and it is saying, "This is what is important. This is what I long for." The vibration already is in my heart, and it brings me forward to the life I want to create.

Speaking of Needs

One of the things that is important to me when I am sharing anything around Nonviolent Communication is having a kind of flexibility around the words and terms that are used to refer to the energy of needs—something that is both an experience and a consciousness. I use the words for needs and values synonymously. Depending on the context, I may use the words "need" or "value" or even the phrases "what matters to me" or "what is precious to me."

When I use any of these words, I am speaking about something that is qualitative, not quantitative. This points to the fundamental distinction in NVC between needs and strategies. If I say, "I have a need for honesty," it's the same thing as saying, "I value honesty." "I have a need for authenticity" is the same thing as "I value authenticity" or "Authenticity matters to me." So, when I am experiencing authenticity or honesty—whether I receive it from you or I'm expressing it—that experience is something I feel in an embodied way. It is not just a concept.

If at any moment, I connect with a longing in my heart, that longing is a vibration of something that is already whole and present. It is not something that is in the future as an outcome. For example, if I say, "I want to be in an intimate relationship. I want to be close to someone. I don't have that in my life," I wouldn't say, "I long for an intimate relationship." I would say, "I long for intimacy." The form this might take—the "strategy," as we say in NVC—would be to have a specific person share a period of my time or my life with me.

Whenever we express ourselves authentically, the challenge can be to stay self-connected while speaking. My understanding of why that happens is that authenticity requires a deeper, felt sense of vulnerability that is often unfamiliar. We aren't trained or conditioned in how to give expression to our vulnerability, so, that's a capacity that we can develop over time. When this challenge occurs, I suggest suspending the desire to speak and, instead, just dwelling in the energy that is present, feeling it without speaking. As we dwell in the energy of vulnerable authenticity, we begin to trust it more. Our minds have been conditioned to describe the experience and then to express that description rather than allowing the experience itself to find the words. I suggest asking yourself, "Can I allow my experience to find the words?" It doesn't matter what the words are...sometimes, what comes is just a sound. Trust the authentic self and allow it to express, however it wants to come out.

Practices and Processes

I offer guided meditations and other practices in each chapter of this book to help you cultivate a spiritual practice. These processes have been structured in every way as invitations to inner exploration. Each meditation and practice is based on what I have discovered as maps to these inner landscapes, and they have the potential for deeper connection to this mystery and intelligence that I want to follow. My hope for you is to trust in your own practice, sense what is valuable for you, and trust in that. This is what I do.

As you use these practices, you will grow in the foundational capacity to be with and allow your experience. This capacity is at the heart of all the processes I offer. I recommend first developing the basic capacity to be present by processing with something that is not intense as you are developing the ability to be with higher intensity.

My intention is to engage in these practices in my life all the time. Every moment, I want to remember to feel myself, feel the energy in my life, the life in my body. There's a core principle in all of the processes I offer: *Whatever arises, you allow it, embrace it, and love it, just as it is*. You open to whatever you encounter, allow it to be there, and bring compassion to it.

Receiving my cancer diagnosis in 2018 was a profound and intense experience. But something happened that was almost miraculous. A pathway opened for me, and immediately I felt (beyond a surface fear) an enormous gratitude for life...for what life was and is and continues to offer me. This gratitude was so powerful that it was a theme that lasted throughout my whole experience. And at the same time, I was able to open and greet the experience. It wasn't very painful, but there was an intense energy of exhaustion. And I just allowed myself to feel completely tired and exhausted. I don't know how to explain the many dimensions of experiencing that accompanied me through this time except that I am grateful for the practices I've discovered and used in my life and that they were there and available for me to be with myself, to allow myself to feel whatever I felt.

PRACTICE: A Meditation on the Quality of Love

You might want to record the following meditation first and then play it to guide you. Note that the "…pause…" is an invitation to give yourself time to notice and be with whatever is present.

Let's begin:

I invite you to close your eyes and bring into your awareness someone you love, someone you deeply care about, someone you highly regard. Vividly imagine this person. Perhaps imagine being with this person, exchanging words, sharing energy.

…pause…

As you are imagining this person—bringing them into your heart—just allow yourself to feel the energies and the feelings that arise as you hold this person in your awareness.

Can you feel the emotions that are connected to this quality of love and deep care?

…pause…

Do you notice the body and how the body vibrates…the sensations that your body feels in the quality and energy of love or care or regard?

...pause...

If anything else arises, just allow that. If something that is unpleasant or uncomfortable or painful arises, just notice and allow that.

...pause...

Notice if love is taking other shapes. Maybe it takes the form of support. Maybe it takes the form of belonging or beauty. Or maybe it takes the form of other qualities connected to this care, this love that you have.

...pause...

Notice if there's something in your mind. Maybe there's some thinking...thoughts or a story that is arising in your mind as you are invited into this process. If this happens, just observe it.

...pause...

And as best you are able, stay connected to feeling this quality, this energy of love or care and, if you can, just slowly remove the other person from this experience. Gently relax your focus on the person and allow yourself to feel just the love itself. Feel it in your body. See if you can breathe with it...flow with it.

...pause...

Although this love came alive with this other person, is it possible to feel the energy of the love just by itself?

...pause...

Allow yourself to keep breathing fully.

...pause...

Embodying this quality—which is something of a lens of your heart—I invite you to expand your view beyond this initial person to other people. Can you see others through this energy of love?

...pause...

Now, can you see your community...your country...all human beings with this energy?

...pause...

Staying as connected with this energy as you can, allow yourself to dwell in the present moment...breathing...

...pause...

And now, slowly bring your awareness forward into your outer environment.

You may wish to journal from your experience.

PRACTICE: Expressing from the Heart

This practice can be done alone by journaling with yourself or by sharing aloud with someone else. If you are doing this practice alone, you might want to record the invitations first and then play your recording, pausing where it says, "...pause..." to receive and then respond to each one.

If you are processing with another person (the practices offered in this book will refer to this person as your "partner"), they can offer the invitations and then wait as a silent witness while you share your responses aloud.

Don't rush through this practice. Take the time you need to connect with each invitation so you can fully receive it. Connect to what's alive and then share (and perhaps write down) what arises.

Let's begin:

I invite you to bring your attention to your body and to your breath. Relax and breathe.

...pause...

Think of something you have wanted to say to someone but that you have not said. What you want to say doesn't have to be painful or even about an unmet need. It can be about anything you've wanted to express but haven't yet said.

…pause…

Write down (or tell your partner) what you could say in a way that you believe would have the best chance of being heard. Keep this brief. Rather than going into details, just choose the essentials you want to communicate.

…pause…

Now, silently reflect on the value, need, or longing that underlies your desire to express this.

…pause…

When you are ready, write down (or share with your partner) what you have discovered, using one word or a short phrase.

...pause...

Remember a time when this value/need/longing was present, and it was met. Allow yourself to connect to what it felt like, to experience the energy that was present in you when the need was met back then.

...pause...

This is more than a mental exercise. It's a memory of the embodied experience of this need that was fulfilled. Remembering is a way to support your connection with the fullness of this need in the present moment, even though it happened in the past. Notice what is alive in you at this moment.

...pause...

Write down (or share with your partner) your bodily experience of this value, need, or longing in its fullness.

…pause…

Now, from this place of dwelling in the fullness of the need, write down (or say out loud to your partner) what you could say to this other person who you've wanted to express to but have not. Don't worry about the words, instead, allow the energy of your heart to speak for you.

…pause…

When you have completed your sharing, if you are practicing with a partner, you can switch roles.

Compassionate presence allows the knotted form we feel as constriction to unfold. We do not make it unfold. It unfolds naturally because that is the wisdom of life itself. Healing happens in the presence of love. It is the nature of life unfolding.

CHAPTER 2

I have learned that human beings are not searching for philosophies, even though it may seem that way sometimes. We are searching for something we can trust. And when we find ourselves in the midst of change, the philosophies are like a broken crutch. They do not hold us up. What supports us is a force, an energy, a vortex of love that expresses through us as warmth, creativity, service, and compassion.

The journey Home is not an ideological experience. It takes place in the heart, in the great stream of feelings which flow through us. Our return to truth is a return to simplicity and not to cosmic information.
~ Stephen Schwartz²

The way I conceptualize living into the principles of Nonviolent Communication, I have termed a two-fold, spiritual life practice. Every moment in my life, my intention is to live in the passion of my life energy and my life force. And at every moment when my life force is obstructed, I want to bring compassion to it.

I see two primary and encompassing processes in life, and they are integrated, intermingled, and interwoven with one another. They both have a primary orientation to life that is towards the already-present fullness within us. This is different from our learned orientation towards lack, which I explored in the last chapter. I call these two integrated streams "passion and compassion."

The first stream of my life practice is that I intend to live in this fullness of the life energy, to embody what I care about, to live the passion and the energy of my needs. I want to intend this moment by moment, in the flow of life that changes, varies, and comes and goes. I want to live according to this intention and this energy. I want to live with the qualities of presence, authenticity, compassion, and freedom, and I want to live this in my relationships.

Inevitably, I will experience moments of life when this flow is blocked; moments when I am not in the flow. When I am not in the flow, it is usually because of a conscious or an unconscious reaction to something someone said or some other life event. This is when I bring in the second stream of my life practice. When I'm in reaction; when I'm contracted; when I'm in judgment; when I am disconnected; then my intention is to bring compassion to these parts of myself and my experiencing.

The obstruction of the life force is the result of our conditioning and our trauma. It manifests as judgments and as the reactive experiences of fear, anger, overwhelm, and violence of all forms. In relating to these obstructions, we've learned to judge and make an enemy of these parts of ourselves, stuck in the orientation of problems and lack. The compassion stream of the two-fold life practice helps us meet and welcome these obstructions with curiosity, openness, care, and warmth. Through my life practice, I know that compassion sees all obstructions as life longing for fulfillment. When I follow this path, I experience the energy of compassion restoring wholeness and reconnecting me to the underlying beauty of life.

The compassion stream is akin to one of the first principles of Nonviolent Communication (NVC). I remember Marshall Rosenberg sharing that all violence—whether physical, emotional, or psychological—is a tragic expression of needs. A different way of conveying the same principle is that every expression, even one full of judgment, has at its heart nothing other than our life reaching for life.

What I love about this practice is that it's simple. It is not necessarily easy to do, but it's a simple practice. I don't need to be analytical about life. I develop and cultivate passion, the energy of my needs, or compassion when I'm experiencing judgment, suffering, or any other contracted experience.

Orienting Towards Life

There are certain principles I want to remember in my spiritual practice. What matters to me, what I truly long for, is always a "yes" in relationship to life. I want to find the "yes" behind any inner "no" that I experience. For me, a "no" points to what is wrong or what is missing. "No" is an expression of lack rather than of the life force. It might take a while for me to explore and transform the nature of this "no," and, maybe in the process, some conditioned thought will be revealed. However, I'm not trying to find the conditioned thought or trauma. I simply want to open my awareness to see what's revealed when I listen to the energy of the "no." What is this part of me saying? What is this part feeling? What is it scared of? And behind that, what is the "yes?"

When I am connected to the "yes," I am connected to life. A primary focus of this teaching is the development, growth, and cultivation of a foundational embodied consciousness of life and an energetic connection with the life impulse we call human needs. This life impulse shows up in me as "I value belonging," or "I long for understanding," or "What matters to me is being seen," or "I want freedom." These are all different expressions of how the life force shows up as "yes" in me. I always receive any of these as a "yes" and as being connected with life.

The fundamental life force that contains everything is love. It takes the different shapes of all the other qualities: love in the form of support, love in the form of consideration, love in all forms and qualities of our needs. Another shape the life force takes is freedom: my power to choose, moment by moment, whatever it is that I am choosing. I can put my attention on lack (such as habitual, reactive thinking) and the orientation towards "no," or I can put my attention on life (an inner bodily connection to what is alive in the moment) and the orientation towards "yes."

These practices are not always easy, but they always have a clear intention. Whatever arises, love it. Whatever arises, allow it. Whatever arises, be with it. Most importantly, whatever arises, hold the intention to be aware and sensitive to that inner life, to that inner flow of energy and feeling. This is the guiding intentionality of my two-fold, spiritual life practice of passion and compassion. In every moment of life, I want to be fully present. I want to live in my needs and my values. I want to express them. I want to regard other people with the awareness that these people matter to me. This is one of the primary capacities I develop in the work that I call Living Compassion.

In its initial stages, this orientation towards life can be seen as a conceptual framework and used as a guide, as something to remember. Even if I don't experience it immediately, I can remember, "Okay, this is what I am experiencing, this difficulty, this problem, this contraction, pain, and suffering. Can I remember to bring a particular quality of awareness to meet it rather than resist it?"

I don't know anybody who never gets triggered. I haven't gotten to this place. However, when it happens, I want to find the beauty in it. I want to encompass and welcome the life that is in the energy of that contraction.

In every moment, I want my orientation to be towards life, not towards problems or beliefs that something is wrong or toward lack in any form. At those times when I am not experiencing the fullness of life, if my intention is to remember to orient myself towards life, to that which is the already-present fullness, then this tuning in becomes my guide and I don't tend to get so sidetracked.

Directing Consciousness

One of the ways I see this cultivation of consciousness is when I embody it. I see that I can direct my life force, and it is my conscious agency that directs my focus towards my life force. What I call "the energy of the heart" is not just a feeling energy. There's an intelligence to the energy, and I can cultivate my ability to direct this intelligent energy of my being, or of my heart, in very specific ways. This directing of my consciousness directs my energy. One of the specific ways I cultivate this ability is when I bring my intention and, therefore, my energy, to distinguish between what I observe and what I think about what I observe—my evaluations, my stories, and my judgments. This directing of my consciousness is one way I conceptualize living NVC.

We are continually putting our attention on something in ourselves, in our inner awareness and inner experience, and on our outer experiencing: in our relationships and in life. If meditation is directing attention, you can say that we are always meditating on something. The question is, "What are we meditating? Where is our attention? What is the quality of our attention?"

Implied in these questions is that if we're not meditating on something focused, directed, conscious, and present, then we are meditating on the relatively unconscious habituation that can be seen as being safe but limiting. Our attention is focused on some form of habitual, relatively unconscious thinking and acting.

On the other hand, we can choose to have a conscious, deliberate intention to focus our attention on present-moment aliveness and authenticity. The beautiful thing I see about the work of Living Compassion is that it is a map for journeying into presence and deep authenticity. In our essence, we are beings who are living in a life flow. We are in a current, like an electrical current, although this life current is deeper and more subtle. This current of life is a manifestation of our beingness. It is our life moving through love.

Inherent Fullness

When we say a need has been "unmet," that language can be problematic for people. "I need something" implies I'm lacking it. That's not what I mean by "need." The way I know that a need is not fulfilled is that I am conscious of it. This means I am conscious of my life force.

What I mean by "need" is that there is a vibration of my heart that tells me what matters to me. That vibration of my heart is already full. The spiritual practice of this is to hold my needs, my longings, with passion but the outcome lightly, meaning I'm not grasping it. I'm not attached to the outcome. If I am attached to the outcome, then I'm experiencing lack. I am orientated towards lack. Another way to say this is that what I am experiencing isn't in alignment with my life force. There's a misalignment, a dissonance. I want to be primarily oriented towards the life force, living oriented toward my life force in every moment. This is the power of what guides me. Moment by moment, I experience life as dissonance, resonance, dissonance, resonance, fulfillment, unfulfillment. But none of my experience is based on lack. It is based on life, which is inherently full.

My orientation when I communicate needs is absolutely essential. When I say, "I have a need for ____" or "I have a longing for ____," it doesn't mean I am lacking it. It means there is an impulse of my nature that I am tuning into. There is no lack present. The language of life helps me to communicate this. When I say, "What matters to me is understanding," this doesn't mean I am lacking understanding. The impulse of understanding wants to emerge and I'm wanting it to do that so I can live the impulse of understanding with you. I want us to live it together, bringing what can be called the "universal essence" into the interpersonal relationship forum. When I have my primary focus on connecting, by which I mean that I am revealing my authenticity and receiving yours, I am less likely to be attached to a specific need being met. Holding our needs passionately and the outcome lightly is one of the central aspects of living this consciousness in relationships. We can then meet in the space of mutuality.

Observations and Needs

Nonviolent Communication cultivates discernment that supports the development of many important skills and consciousness. I encourage practice with them all, and I will elaborate on some.

One important skill to develop is the ability to distinguish between what I am observing and what I am thinking in evaluative and judgmental terms. When I can differentiate my judgments from my observations, I am freed to then enter into a relative openness and vulnerability. Being open and vulnerable is another way of saying, "I am in an undefended state with respect to what I am experiencing." If I am in a defended and protected state, this means that, to some degree, I am in my patterns of judging and evaluating.

In a direct relationship to the stimulus or the observation, my experience is no longer mediated by my thinking, my judgments, and my evaluations. In this way NVC helps me cultivate openness. I can go directly to my heart. In relationship to what others may say, my awareness of needs guides me to ask myself, "What matters to me? What am I needing in relation to this?" Further steps take me into the relationship space, where we invite each other into a mutual experience. I show up, you show up, this is what matters to me, and I hear what matters to you. Out of this space, we can move forward into collaborative action, where we meet each other in our requests.

A basic principle of NVC is that people are always and only expressing the life in them. However, sometimes they do not do this in a clear way. For many people who are new to NVC (and even people who have been around NVC for a while), attempting to connect an experience to a need is often head-centered. They connect to what the word "need" means rather than to their body's intelligence, making the shift from their head to their heart.

A distinction I find so important is that we can think about what the needs and values are, and in this way, needs can make some sort of logical sense. But when, instead, we stay with our sensations, it can be like walking across a threshold into a different possibility. Remaining open and waiting in this openness, something much larger and more encompassing can emerge that is beyond the mind. One of the reasons I've developed Living

Compassion processes and practices is to help people connect to the embodiment of need energy rather than to just the word that describes it.

Acknowledging Our Feelings

Another important capacity developed by NVC is my ability to experience authentic feelings and then to connect with my needs and longings so I can embody and communicate them. One of the fundamental steps in working with the complexity of feelings is to acknowledge that I am feeling something, that something is going on inside me. This requires self-honesty, even if I can't name what I am feeling.

The capacity to feel and acknowledge what I am feeling is such an important element of being self-connected and self-aware. And I must be able to notice what I am feeling to convey to another person the degree of authenticity I am living.

"Feelings" and "emotions" are two words that are often used interchangeably, but they can also be used differently. If I have a sensation, my experience of that sensation can be that I am feeling something. And if there's an emotional feeling, then it's a different kind of experience. Both are feelings: either an emotional feeling or a feeling of sensation. I don't think there's an absolute definition for this word; it depends on who is speaking and how they are defining "feeling." I like to qualify what I am describing in this way: "I'm having an emotional feeling," meaning I am experiencing certain emotions like warmth, joy, happiness, relief. I describe a feeling of energetic flow in my body as a physical sensation or a felt sense. My experience of this energy is that "I am feeling it," but what I am experiencing is not an emotional feeling.

Defended Feelings and Anger

There is a distinction between what I call "reactive feelings" and more heart-connected feelings, which I call "non-reactive" or undefended, vulnerable feelings. For example, it might be that underneath an experience of anger I am feeling scared. The anger is a way to protect myself from the more vulnerable feeling of fear. It also might be that my fear has a story that projects into the future and predicts that something is going to happen.

I call a number of defended feelings "whole experiences" because they include thinking or a story and are, therefore, more than emotions. I see anger as a valid, authentic experience, but it is reactive in that it usually carries within it some sort of judgment or enemy image or projection onto the other person or onto myself. So, the evaluative thought or story in that judgment is not a feeling, yet it is a component of the "whole experience" we call anger.

I want to recognize that anger is authentic and that there are two different streams to experiencing it. One stream can be expressed as "I am angry because something matters to me, and it is that which matters to me that I'm needing and valuing." I want to remember that anger is about my needs. If I don't remember this, then I'll end up in the other stream, which is of blame and judgment and enemy images whose expression is, "I'm angry because of YOU!" This kind of reactive thinking almost always goes with anger. When I'm angry, I'm going to be in my head, judging the other person. When I am in that state, who's suffering? They aren't; I am.

Marshall Rosenberg pointed out that anger tells us two things. One is that we are going into our heads, where we are creating enemy images that are full of evaluations and judgments. The other thing anger tells us is that there are needs we are not in touch with. To help be present with the intensity of anger, to create some inner space, and ultimately to transform anger, we can acknowledge and name our judgments and enemy images and then connect to our needs, to the energy of what matters to us. Transformation may not come easily, but at least this process

51

provides a map to navigate the inner territory of our anger.

It can be challenging being with the energy of someone who is expressing their anger in front of me. They are angry about something and expressing what's important to them. It takes quite a focus to connect to what matters to them when I'm being stimulated by their anger. Some deep conditioning in me tells me, "It's dangerous! I don't want to be around it. I get scared when someone is angry." The more I engage in my inner work, when this fear has been stimulated, the more I am able to be increasingly present to the person when they express anger in front of me. It depends on many things. Do I have the space to pause? Can I listen to the person's anger and hear what they are angry about? Can I let them know that I hear what they are angry about—that something matters to them—and reflect even just that?

The important skill of transforming my own anger and of approaching the anger of others is remembering that there is always an orientation toward life that I can choose. If I'm angry, it is because something matters. If I am angry, can I transform my anger and own or embrace the passion behind it? And then, can I express openly, vulnerably, and tenderly what it is that matters to me? Otherwise, what I am likely to communicate is my judgments, and these will create more defensiveness.

The nature of self-compassion and self-connection is the foundation of our living. It is the foundation of how we communicate. Compassion invites awareness underneath the anger and fear, so I can touch into the more vulnerable parts of my experience.

The Beauty of Needs

Needs are an aspect or an expression of the energy of life. They arise from life, expressing the requisites of life necessary to sustain itself. We experience the beauty of a need when we are in contact with the quality of its energy. This reaching to contact the energy of the need is an aspect of wanting to nurture and extend life. Holding our awareness on living from this divine life impulse is the intention to nurture and extend the life that is expressed within the energy of every essential living need.

There are two meanings to the phrase, "meet our needs." One meaning is to request something of people, giving them the opportunity to do something to contribute to our well-being. This is a function of action. I (or someone else) will use a strategy—take an action—to fulfill a need.

Another way to "meet" a need is to get acquainted with how this need lives in us as an expression of our essence. When we do this, when we touch that need, we are touched by life, and we live the quality of this need in our very being. This is a function of attention. By using our attention, we can become aware of our needs as they live in us. We become acquainted with our needs and, by embracing them, we fully and energetically experience the quality of our needs without regard to their fulfillment.

Developing the ability to focus our attention on and cultivating the intention to connect to the life energy within needs, is one of the most important abilities we develop within Nonviolent Communication. It is the embodied spirituality of NVC. In touch with our essence, we follow the longing, the yearning to experience this quality of the ecstatic flow of life. When we do this, we are in touch with the need in an embodied way, and we experience its qualities, its essence, how it feels when that need is met, and how we experience this "met-ness" in our body, emotions, and in our very being.

PRACTICE: A Guided Meditation to Connect with Fullness

Every need has a quality of wholeness in it. Developing a familiarity with this wholeness is a kind of meditation. By practicing this, we begin to live from the core of these qualities.

The intention of this meditation is to connect to the fullness of life energy through your heart. Although this meditation focuses on the needs for acceptance and trust, this practice can be applied to any need.

You might want to record the meditation first and then play it to guide you. Each time it says, "...pause...," I encourage you to take the time you need to notice and be with whatever is present.

Becoming Centered

Let's begin:

I'd like to invite you to begin by becoming centered, however you do that. You might want to start by noticing your breath...then close your eyes and bring your attention to your body.

…pause…

Feel the sense of awareness in you and around you. As you do this, breathe and notice if you can relax more. This is not a passive relaxation; it's very alert and relaxed.

…pause…

Connect with your reason for being here, your intention for taking time to do this meditation. You also tune into the significance, the importance of you being here, present.

…pause…

Feel your body, solid, sitting in the seat.

Acceptance (or any other need you choose)

Now, take a few minutes to remember a time when you experienced acceptance, perhaps in relation to another person. You might express this to yourself as, "My need for acceptance was met fully" or "I had the experience of being fully accepted by another person."

Remember this experience as vividly as you can. You can even see, visualize, or remember words that were said. Remembering often helps to connect to the energy of the need you are exploring. The most important part of this practice is to feel the embodiment of this specific quality of acceptance.

…pause…

Now, bring your memory into the present moment. As you remember, do you feel that quality, the actual experience of acceptance? In this quality is there a sort of recognition that all of you is welcomed and accepted? Take a moment to dwell in this feeling, in this energy of a real experience you had.

…pause…

Allow yourself to simply feel that energy of acceptance. Feel it in the body. Notice the emotional feelings that come with this energy. Notice whatever else arises in this process. Just allow it.

…pause…

There may be some tenderness. There may be some painful feelings. Just allow whatever is there to be there. Allow yourself to breathe.

…pause…

Maybe another quality comes into your consciousness, and you can name it. Is there a quality of care? Perhaps a feeling of warmth? Simply allow yourself to dwell and bathe in this energy in your body.

…pause…

Whether your experience is of another person accepting you or you are remembering the experience of extending acceptance towards another person, just stay with it and become familiar with this felt experience.

…pause…

As you slowly bring your attention back, take another moment—with your eyes closed or open—to continue the process a little bit longer.

…pause…

Can you imagine speaking from this energy?

…pause…

Can you imagine speaking to a person, to someone you care about, to someone for whom acceptance matters both ways, giving and receiving?

…pause…

Do you sense an openness? Perhaps a tenderness, a vulnerability as you might reveal yourself to what is very dear to you?

…pause…

Take a few breaths, shift your energy, and allow the energy you've connected with in this practice to stay in you.

You can continue by connecting with the energy of the need for trust (or other need) now or explore trust on another occasion by beginning with the "Becoming Centered" introduction to this practice to bring your awareness into the present moment.

Trust (or any other need you choose)

As you did when connecting with the energy of acceptance, remember an experience, a person, or a relationship in which you experienced, or do experience, trust…whatever the word "trust" means to you. Bring this relationship into your

61

mind right now and imagine it as vividly as possible. Maybe you remember some of the things that were said or done in this relationship.

…pause…

Now, bring the embodied energy of your memory into the present moment. As you remember, do you feel that quality, the actual experience of trust? Take a moment to notice how you feel, how the body feels.

…pause…

Relax into the energy of trust as you are holding the image of this person with whom you experience trust.

…pause…

Perhaps you feel the energy of trust as a longing, as something precious to you, that you long to experience in your relationships.

…pause…

Observe or notice if other qualities are interwoven with trust. Perhaps you sense care, perhaps peace. Maybe there's a feeling of warmth or joy? Whatever arises with the felt energy of trust, allow yourself to relax into it and feel it in your body.

…pause…

Sometimes the mind comes in. Just notice what the narrative, evaluative mind is telling you. Maybe it is saying something about this exercise or about how you're doing or how you're not doing it. In my experience, this part of the mind can be quite persistent and can come up at times that I don't always enjoy. If this happens for you, simply allow it to be there and observe it.

…pause…

Notice if there are other relationships, where you long for trust. Maybe this includes the one you brought into this practice today? Put your focus on the longing in your heart for trust (not the lack of it). Notice your longing arises from the fullness of what you deeply value, what is precious, what is dear to you.

…pause…

Allow yourself to feel whatever comes up.

…pause…

Sometimes sadness comes up because what we long for is not as fully present as we would want.

…pause…

This feeling, this energy is full; it's filled with life. It is an impulse that moves us forward in our life, in our relationships.

…pause…

Just let yourself keep with your breath and allow the energy to move and take different shapes, different intensities.

…pause…

Staying with your breath and slowly coming back into your full space, open your eyes whenever you're ready. Allow yourself to stay connected to this feeling energy as much as you can.

Life Energy

In this meditation, I asked you to connect to a personal relationship because I think it can be easier to relate to acceptance and trust in interpersonal relationships.

Memory is a way to help connect to the energy of a need. For example, if I were doing this process without the memory part, I would say, "Can I connect to the energy of acceptance? What does acceptance feel like when it is being fulfilled for me?" I use these questions to touch the energy.

The important question I ask myself is, "What are the qualities and the energy of my need?" As I sink into this embodied experience of my need, I recognize that this is the energy of my heart. This is life energy. It is life speaking to me and through me, and it is the same life energy I am receiving from others.

What serves us is a deep intuitive trusting and plunging into our own experience of intending to be present with ourselves, with another, in a bodily felt, heart-centered presence.

CHAPTER 3

When your emotional world is alive, it can feel as if you must act urgently to bring relief to the fire within. A familiar sense of overwhelm is present. The panic has returned.

In these moments, slow way down. Rest your tired mind and your achy heart. Descend out of the vivid narrative and into the earthy, muddy ground of your body. Surround the sacred material with your presence and offer safe passage to the temporary, wavelike intensity that is washing through. It is not an enemy but a harbinger of integration.

The inner landscape is being painted by the abandoned ones of your holy nervous system, seeking the light of cohesion and wholeness.

Dare to consider that nothing has gone wrong and that you have not failed. It is only the light of the path, come in a form the mind may never understand. Trust in the holding field of your body.

The beloved is coming to know herself, through the vastness of somatic revelation. She is the artist and your heart her canvas. Your body and your senses are her poetic offering to a weary world.

~ *Matt Licata*[3]

Matt Licata's words are a beautiful, poetic description of a journey into the interior landscape of our inner experience. They contain much of the essence of embodied self-compassion. What is self-compassion? It is a practice that helps us to recognize the blocks or obstructions to the flow of our life energy, restore that flow, and change our relationship to pain. The practice of self-compassion is particularly important when we encounter those difficult situations and we don't know how to recover ourselves and our center.

In the previous chapters, I described the nature of Living Compassion, and I introduced my two primary, encompassing, life-oriented processes. They are two streams of focus—two streams of aliveness, consciousness, and energy. One focus is flowing with the life force and embodying the energy of my *passion* of that which I care about. The other focus is the practice of *compassion*, meeting and welcoming with curiosity, openness, care, and warmth, anything that obstructs this life force.

Passion is the life force, the life energy emanating from that which already is the fundamental unity of life. With passion, my intention is to embody, live, and express the authenticity of my being. I want to dwell in the energy of my heart and a deeply felt sense of what really matters to me. I value truth, honesty, compassion, and nonviolence. I value holding my own needs and my own mattering fully and equally, with myself and with other people. The values I am holding in my heart show up in many different ways. One way to describe them is that they are what I am passionate about or what I deeply care about.

Living into and manifesting my passion in what I care about so I can live with as much fullness and energy as possible is the first stream of my spiritual life practice, and it can be described as along an "in the flow of life" spectrum. I don't know that I am ever fully in this flow with life or that I am ever fully out of it, but when I am living in the energy of my needs, in the energy of my heart, I experience this as a flow. I experience a strength in my energy and a clarity in my mind.

When I am not in this flow—when I encounter a life event that is difficult to experience—and I examine my own internal response in relation to it, the internal characteristic of this experience is one of blocking the flow; I experience an energetic block on a physical level. The purpose of the second stream of my spiritual life practice is to establish and cultivate a relationship of compassion with my pain, in whatever form I am experiencing it. Doing this entails focusing my attention and bringing a particular quality of awareness to be with this contracted constellation of pain.

Living Authenticity

For me, pain is a form of my life force that points to what matters to me. I call this "natural pain." In this undefended relationship with my pain, I experience the fullness of what I value, not the lack of it.

When I move into vulnerable sadness, I am touched by what is precious and beautiful in my heart. This kind of sadness I describe as "sweet pain." This pain is not constricted; it is tender and relaxed. When I get in touch with pure, open-hearted sadness, there is a kind of sinking into it, a relaxing, and a letting go. This sweet and natural pain is absolutely essential to fully living my authenticity. Living with an open heart means living with a broken-open heart. This requires a willingness to feel pain when something I experience isn't in harmony with what I hold dear, as well as a willingness to feel the joy that emerges when there is resonance. When I live with an open heart, pain and joy are equally embraced.

Unless I am in the place where I hold pain and joy as equal, I know I am resisting life in some way. If I want joy more than pain, then I am resisting being fully present in the fullness of my heart in that moment. I want to remember that encompassing presence has a higher order that embraces both pain and joy. When I arrive in this embracing place, I feel the higher order of presence. It is Grace.

To be fully present to life, I must be present to all of life's experiences, pain, and joy. When I am inhabiting this state of presence, I am aware that emotional pain can't hurt me and that it is an inner guide that points me to my heart. When I am seated in my heart, nothing can hurt me there.

Suffering Pain

When I am in pain, what matters to me is my relationship to it. If I have a relationship with my pain where it closes me off and puts me into my reactive and judgmental mind, I call this "suffering pain," rather than natural pain.

Suffering is disconnected from life. It is our thinking that creates our suffering—being caught up in the illusion of whatever we are telling ourselves and believing about the situation and our pain. We suffer when we are separate from our heart and from the authenticity of our needs.

When I am in a suffering state, the nature of my internal experience is contraction. With a physical contraction, I may feel hot, tight, heavy, and sometimes numb (which is also a physical sensation). I may feel the contraction of reactive

73

emotions such as fear and anger or any of their variations and modifications. I may also be contracted in my thinking, which then becomes very narrow and focused on polarizations such as right and wrong, good and bad, power over and power under, submission and rebellion. Suffering pain can also restimulate past trauma with all of its associated stories.

What I want is to remember that pain connects me to my life force, to my needs and my values, and I want to remember that I can choose this orientation to life.

If I am experiencing something I care about in connection with a need that was unfulfilled, I often feel a degree of sadness and grief. This is natural pain arising in response to mourning. When I open myself to feel the natural pain arising when something I deeply care about is unfulfilled, mourning always points me towards the beauty of my needs. Mourning is an essential part of a spiritual practice. If I am not in touch with the beauty, then I am not in fullness. This doesn't mean I have to experience fullness, but this awareness is a useful indication for me.

Intimacy with Our Inner Child

My intention is to live in the present moment and to compassionately embrace my pain. I recognize that all of my deeper pain comes from my young years, and it shows up when it gets triggered. I particularly want to bring compassion to these young, wounded parts of me. I want to open vulnerably to myself and feel the tenderness within me as much as I can. When I do this, I establish an intimate relationship with that young part of me that did not experience what he needed. There is a beautiful, intimate relationship I can generate with this part of me.

I also want to be watchful, and to notice the tendency of this young part to project the inner child's urgency to have needs fulfilled into my current, adult life, and to expect others to meet them. I don't think there's anything "wrong" with doing this, but when I can orient towards my inner, young self, I feel this inner tenderness. I no longer have this compelling sense of grasping, desperation, or deficiency.

Sometimes, I suggest approaching this young part as I would an innocent child who is scared or hurt. This young, innocent part reacts to difficult situations in life by seeking to protect itself because it sees events and situations as dangerous and possibly hurtful or restrictive, as they may have been in the past.

The way I have learned how to transform this kind of deep pain is by turning that inner child around so I face him. Even if this young, wounded part of me is desperately seeking acceptance from others, I know I am the one he deeply needs acceptance from now. He wants to know he is safe with me, and that he matters to me. When I view this part of me as innocent, it awakens compassion and then the constriction begins to relax. In an environment of inner compassion, healing is possible.

Life at the Heart of Pain

The approach to inner compassion carries an intention that is life-centered, not pain-centered. What this means is there is an intention to meet the pain with recognition and compassion. Even though I may not have a direct experience of this intention at the beginning, there is a recognition that life, itself, is at the heart of all pain. At the core of all of my pain is unmet and unfulfilled longings. When I am able to bring a particular quality of awareness to my contracted pain, more internal spaciousness is created.

In the course of life, whenever I encounter another person doing or saying what I don't enjoy—or I experience any event I don't enjoy—as I notice I am being stimulated I want to recognize when there is a painful contraction, a pulling in, and usually an inability to free myself or restore my wholeness. I want to notice I am cutting myself off, or I have a felt sense of being cut off from a relaxed, present flow of energy. Bodily tension and contraction are components of restricting the flow of my energy that I want to recognize. There is also usually a narrative, a story (which sometimes I may not consciously recognize) that shows up in the form of judgments and evaluations and, sometimes, intellectual analysis.

Often when I am scared or angry, I feel the tension in my body. When I feel the reactive emotions of overwhelm or powerlessness, I feel them in my body. The important part of this practice of self-compassion is to recognize and acknowledge my experience of contraction and to simply say to myself, "I'm noticing that my body feels tight in relation to what I just observed. I am sensing an emotion of fear or anger," or whatever the emotion is.

I'm not suggesting you try to relax the tension; that would be a strategy. I'm suggesting that you *bring your attention* to the tension, as it is, without trying to relax it. When I do this, relaxing emerges naturally because the attention creates space. The relaxation, the result, is an emergent, natural process.

Even when I begin this process by scanning my body, there's a recognition that brings with it more internal space between the one who is observing (me) and the observed content of my experience (the tension, emotions, and thoughts). This is the pathway of self-compassion, and it is one of the primary skills that I cultivate in this compassion practice.

The Practice of "Being With"

One of the first elements in the practice of self-compassion is pausing and breathing. When I focus my awareness, my breath helps me to slow down so I can encounter the physiological nuances of the contraction and my automatic thoughts.

Another element in the practice of self-compassion is holding a clear intention to "be with" whatever I am experiencing. I've been conditioned to try to get away from pain. If I'm feeling something painful, my conditioning tells me, "I want to feel better. I want to escape the pain; I want to alleviate it." With a lot of psychological and emotional reactive pain, this process of moving away from pain is counter to self-compassion because it is a way of resisting my experience. In the act of avoiding it, I consciously or unconsciously judge the pain as bad or wrong.

The intention of compassion is completely different from this resistance. Rather than attempting to get away from any pain, suffering, or discomfort, my intention is to allow it just to be there. Although this might sound simple, it can be challenging in practice. The intention of self-compassion is simply to let the nature of this experience be present, to allow it to be within my experiencing. Although being with the experience is a skill, when I am able to do this, I can begin to feel an almost immediate relief, even if just a little bit.

Developing my capacity to be with my experience transforms my relationship to the pain. Rather than resisting pain, I begin to allow it to be. I tell myself, "It's okay to feel this," even if a part of me is railing against feeling it and is convinced that it is not okay. When I enter into the experience of resistance, the parts of me I resist become enemies, they become something I am trying to get away from. The spiritual part of my being, which is compassion, wants to befriend these inner enemies.

I have found it very helpful to identify and relate with the different aspects of my being. For example, If I'm feeling scared, I want to change the language so that, instead of saying, "I'm scared," I want to say, "There's *a part of me* that is scared. There is an energy in my being that is fearful." Self-compassion embraces all parts of me.

The more I engage in a practice of compassion, the more compassionate awareness becomes strengthened. If the nature and the quality of my experience don't relax as quickly as I expect it to, then the part of my mind that gets impatient might say, "I'm trying this, but it is not working!" One of the most important capacities to develop within myself is patience, which is a form of self-trust. Compassion, awareness, patience, and self-trust are some of the many capacities I develop as I practice inner compassion.

Self-compassion can also be called a form of inner empathy. As my consciousness focuses on these inner parts of myself, I become curious about them. I begin to want to find out more. "What is it that is in the fear?" I may invite the fear to speak to me. "What are you scared of? What is the story in the fear? What am I telling myself about the fear?" As I do this, I open up a space for inner dialogue so I can listen deeply to these parts of myself rather than trying to avoid them. When I try to get past my fears, my reactions, my frustration, my overwhelm...what

I am doing is pushing them to the margins of my awareness so I won't acknowledge them. Any marginalized parts of me will continue to affect the quality of my experience, even if it appears as though I have escaped them.

Self-compassion can be seen as a form of gathering all of the parts of myself that I've pushed away. Now I invite them and, as I welcome them, I begin to feel a warmth and a tenderness towards these parts of myself. A quality of care begins to be generated. As I move through these protective parts of myself, I may feel more vulnerability.

Vulnerability opens the door to feel the mourning or grief underneath the fear and anger, which are more protected states of feeling. Compassion is a process of transforming; as these parts transform, they become softer, they relax, and they become open.

The principle that I return to again and again is that at the very heart of my pain is the quality of life, the quality of beauty, which usually takes the form of unfulfilled needs, unfulfilled longings. Something I invite people to experience is that the beauty of this need is present, whether or not it is being fulfilled. It's a different experience when it's not being fulfilled than when it is, but the underlying beauty, for me, is the most important part of the experience.

Transformation

One of the principles of this practice is that it is experientially an embodied awareness and not an intellectual process. The practice is not something I "think about."

Pain can never be healed by an idea. It can never be healed by adjusting our thoughts or a conceptual understanding of what is going on. Pain can only be healed by coming to it directly and attending to it as it is and not as we want it to be. Now, healing does not mean the pain is gone. Pain is not gone, it is transformed. The very

energy that lies inside the pain is the energy that we want.
~ *Stephen Schwartz*[4]

If a person says something to me that my mind receives as a harsh judgment or as hurtful, I want to notice that this is a judgment arising in me. Something is said, and I have this painful impact on my body. I not only feel something in my body, I also feel something in my emotions. Initially, I might feel angry, and I may experience judgment in my mind. The form that the painful, reactive experience takes is modified by the thinking that I have if I'm judging. It has this emotional suffering pain. But when I focus my attention in a welcoming way on the parts of me that are contracted, the "it" I am approaching—that whole reality or constellation of inner experiencing that I call pain—transforms. To "trans-form" means that the formation of the contraction changes. The essence of the energy of pain is the same, but its shape is transmuted, so to speak.

For example, When I stay with my anger and look underneath it, I may recognize that I'm telling myself that this person is wrong and inconsiderate. As I stay with this recognition, and as I tune into my heart, I feel hurt as a tender and undefended pain. The pain shows me what I value and what I care about. And, when I tune into my value for being considered with care, for being seen and being understood, I recognize that these are the values and the energy that are behind the pain and hurt. This deeper exploration then transforms my initial experience of judgment and anger into the energy that I so value. In my vulnerability and attuned with my heart's longing, natural sadness and grief may arise as well as the need to mourn.

Transcendence

I want to take a moment to clarify the distinction I have between transformation and transcendence, as many people find these confusing. There are a couple of meanings of the word "transcendence." According to certain spiritual practices, if I transcend, the material I'm transcending is still available in my unconscious as the shadow or the dark side that I repress. I am not particularly interested in that kind of transcendence.

However, there is another process of transformation that allows me to transcend: differentiation from what I am identified with. If I am identified with my suffering, these constellations of energies that keep me in the reactive state, then I want to bring compassion to my reactive thinking and allow it to transform. In this case, transcendence is actually differentiation. If I transcend my evaluative thinking, then I can reside in the observational mode. I'm more empowered. Now empowered, I can allow the transformation of that which I've differentiated from. Eventually, this process allows me to connect more to the fullness of what is the heart of the pain that is in my suffering in the first place.

In essence, a spiritual life practice transforms where and how we center our attention and energy. This means reclaiming our power from dependence on the external world: our things, circumstances in our environment, and the opinions of other people. We discover the source of our strength and presence.

The attention and energy of living—our center of gravity —then transforms and connects us to our heart and soul'. We can then live a soul-centered life. We make an inner move from reacting to the exterior reality to abiding in the power and clarity of consciousness. We allow the inner qualities to be a guide to living and engaging in life.

PRACTICE: Compassionately Embracing

You might want to record the meditation first and then play it to guide you. Note that the "...pause..." is an invitation to give yourself time to notice and be with whatever is present.

Let's begin:

I'd like to invite you into a guided process. Let's pause for the moment… breathing…and slowly allow your inner felt experience, whatever it is… just to be… just as it is. As we breathe, we create a spaciousness.

…pause…

If there is any pain, instead of resisting the painful contraction by reacting to a story, interpretations, or any thinking that causes the constriction, allow the breathing to relax the body… and allow the space.

…pause…

Sense that there is room for this inner feeling experience to be. There is room for this feeling to be. There's nothing wrong or right about this feeling. There is nowhere to go, nothing to fix. You are okay just as you are. You are welcoming instead of resisting the feeling experience.

…pause…

Feelings are energy flowing through the body as sensory, emotional realities. Life energy is flowing through you. It is not right or wrong, appropriate or inappropriate. Everything you feel is life seeking to flow, just wanting to be. As you allow this, vulnerability may arise.

…pause…

Notice if you are having a tight, constricting experience the more you do this. If you can open to any constriction, perhaps you can view this vulnerable part of you as a very young part, a very innocent part.

…pause…

If there is a painful feeling, notice…is there a wanting or a quality of longing? Can you feel the longing?

…pause…

As you feel the longing energy, can you sense this longing is for something that is precious? Perhaps for something that relaxes and is deeply comforting? Perhaps you long for love or for a loving presence in which you can relax and feel safe, knowing you are held with care and tenderness?

…pause…

As you continue this practice, you can let yourself relax into the flow of your breathing… gently allowing this life energy of feeling to flow.

…pause…

Maybe you even feel the sacredness of this energy. Can you notice that this energy is bigger than you? It is life's energy moving through you like a river. There's a sense of strength and clarity in the presence of this feeling as you relax into it and allow it to gently hold you and encompass you.

…pause…

There is a deep beauty in this living quality and feeling. You are allowing the beauty to be. You are feeling the energetic quality of this beauty...staying with this...you are giving yourself time to feel the energy of what is precious.

...pause...

Dwelling and resting in the energy of what is precious...breathing and extending it to your entire body, to every cell in your body, to each limb, to the tips of your fingers and your toes...and beyond...let this experience extend into the room you are in...and let it expand out into the field...touching and imbuing everyone you can see and sense, everyone you can imagine, everyone in the entire world.

...pause...

I invite you to stay and dwell in this feeling. Relax any thinking about it. You can use this practice regardless of what you are experiencing inside, whether it's painful or not, just allowing whatever it is.

…pause…

When you are ready, you can open your eyes.

PRACTICE: Integrating Inner and Outer Experience, a Paired Process

When we are living a non-resistant, non-judgmental, compassionate relationship to others, the world, and life, we are integrating our inner and outer experiences.

This practice helps me to remember compassionate awareness: what I call "bringing attention to whatever arises." As I move through one phase or step of this process, it may shift my experience. Then I may move into another experience, but the thoughts and reactive feelings come up again. Whatever arises, I stay with or return to it and be with it.

I acknowledge that this is what is arising in this moment.

Although there are steps to the following process, there is no notion of progressing from one step to the next in the usual way we were conditioned to think. Our mind might say, "Oh, I did this step and this step, so why am I back to an earlier step again?" That could be how our mind evaluates this process, but that is not how integration works, in my experience.

This is an organic process and I stay with my aliveness, its organicity, and unpredictability. I stay with life. It may be that this experience is telling me that I'm needing to attend to it more. Maybe I am needing more time, more spaciousness. This is how the process of life works, too. A new and unexpected dimension arises and, if it is real and genuine, I feel it, then I trust it. It confirms in me the mystery of life and my surrender to it. It shows me—it guides me—into these completely unpredictable spaces that are so alive.

There are two roles in the processes below: the speaker shares what comes up in each numbered step and the receiver silently listens to the speaker. Allow a certain amount of time for one person to practice both Parts A and B before switching roles.

Begin by choosing who will speak first and who will receive first (and speak second).

If you are the first speaker, start slowly, taking time to connect with your experience at each step before sharing with your partner what comes up in you.

When you are the receiver—the empathic witness—be as fully present as you can, receiving the energy in the words that are shared by the speaker. As the receiver, listen in silence or reflect what is shared if the speaker requests reflection.

Part A: The Inner Experience

Choose a stimulus in your life and share what it is with your partner.

Breathe. As you put your attention on your stimulus, focus your awareness on your body.

…pause…

Simply be with the experience, whatever it is. Allow it to be, just as it is. Just sit with it. A metaphor I often use is of an inner room, your inner living room, and these parts of the experience are your guests. You sit with them. You don't have to do anything. You don't even have to engage them. Just sit with them.

…pause…

Notice and identify any thinking, stories, or judgments that arise in your mind. Simply notice them. This is an observing process. Then share them aloud with your partner.

Focus on your body's sensations and your feelings. Notice any intensity and pain and allow yourself to be with it to the degree that you can. Notice you are engaging in a relationship with this pain or intensity.

…pause…

Sense into, and inquire, "What is this energy longing for?" Is there a need, a value, something you long for in this energy? You may sense something, and it may not have words. Or it may have words such as, "This energy is longing for love" or "In this energy, I sense that I am wanting cooperation and engagement." Connect to the energy of the longing, whatever it is.

…pause…

While connecting to the energy, feel it in your body. Dwell in the felt sensing of your need.

…pause…

Now, share your experience with your partner.

Part B: Integration

Focus your attention once again on the outer stimulus or event. Take time to notice that your awareness is now on the outer event.

...pause...

Now focus your attention back on your inner experience.

...pause...

Notice your awareness is holding your outer and inner observing at the same time, but you are also holding them each as distinct. There is the outer event...and then there is the inner experience.

...pause...

Now continue to alternate your attention between them. Focus on your inner experience (whatever you are experiencing in this moment) and then shift your focus to the outer event. Move back and forth between the two in this way a few times. Allow yourself to experience whatever emerges from moving back and forth.

...pause...

As you near the end of this process, notice if there is a request you have of yourself as you are connected to this energy. Is there a request of yourself that comes from the energy itself?

What serves us is a deep, intuitive trusting in life, and a plunging into our own bodily-felt experience with the clear intention for heart-centered presence with ourselves and with another.

Chapter 4

When the truth of love comes, when the real intimacy arises between human beings and the universe itself, that intimacy and that truth are felt. They aren't known conceptually. They arise through the body. So, when we speak of turning to God, when we speak of turning to the infinite one, when we talk of ending separation, they may be ideas and hopefully those ideas serve as inspiration to go on. But the real prayer, the real movement is one in which we turn the attention to the body. Because it is in the body and only in the body that the bliss of union is going to be felt. And not in the mind.

In some very real sense, the mind is totally transformed by a return of the attention to the heart. It becomes a different instrument altogether. It isn't gone, but the function we have assigned to the mind, in our separated state is no longer a useful function at all. The oppressive veil of thought dissolves.

And in its place, we find that the eyes open into the spaciousness of the heart. The ears open into the spaciousness of the heart. The tongue, the sense of touch. All life instead of being filtered through a sensory mechanism caught in thought, redesigned, and then experienced is suddenly experienced directly through the heart.

And it does not encounter density. But rather encounters a lucid open space, in which nothing is caught in definition. Nothing is caught in the past. Nothing is caught in the confines of imposed reality, but is rather allowed to move and change.
~ Stephen Schwartz[5]

Cultivating our observing awareness, and increasing our understanding of the thinking mind, are two elements I find to be essential in the work of Living Compassion and Nonviolent Communication. This quote from Stephen Schwartz expresses something important and eloquent in relation to the work we are doing and to its essential, spiritual aspect.

What stands out for me in this reading, and what I'd like to emphasize, has to do with the functioning of the thinking mind when it's in a separated state. Thought can be one of the obstacles to fully connecting. The kind of thoughts and thinking patterns that become obstacles are those that arise when we are in judgment, when we are evaluating, and when we are in analytical and intellectual thought, separate from the body.

In contrast, the kind of thoughts Stephen talks about in this quote are those that arise when we are centered in our consciousness and fully experiencing life from dwelling in the heart. Thought doesn't go away; it is transformed. Its function changes and thought becomes an instrument of the heart. When I am connected to my heart, whether I am feeling some intense experience or not, the thoughts that arise in my mind ring true. A clarity and a deep "Yes" arise that I feel in my being. This is what I call "inspired thought." The thought in and of itself isn't necessarily a unified, embodied experience, but it can lead and inspire me into cultivating and living in this way.

For example, if I recognize that I'm innocent, that we all are innocent, this doesn't necessarily mean I'm going to experience someone's innocence when they say something that stimulates pain in me. But what this recognition of innocence does is it serves as an inner guidepost. I can say to myself, "Ah, I remember I am innocent. I remember the other person is innocent. What does that mean?" This inner dialogue inspires me to listen and find their innocence in what they are saying and look for my own innocence in my reaction. Inspired thought becomes a guide, making this process of recognition and inner dialogue very useful for me.

The Nature of Mind

It is important to understand the nature of the thinking mind when it is in a separated state and to recognize when separation has occurred. When we can recognize how our thinking mind is in separation, then we are able to make a more conscious choice with regard to it.

Some of the characteristics of the thinking mind are that it filters and mediates experience, so we do not experience life directly, but indirectly. When we are in a separated state, our mind distorts and filters experience. In this state, our mind is influenced by the life experiences that we carry within our system that were consciously or unconsciously created by our mind. We know when the thinking mind is separated from the body because it fears the unknown; it is uncomfortable with the unknown. Two different aspects influence the tendency of the mind to mediate and distort. One is that all the traumatic and painful experiences we've had become internalized beliefs that then have a mediating function. The second important aspect of the mind to understand is that it creates identity—or we can say, the mind creates self-identity—built from a conditioned pattern of experiences that we then take ourselves to be. When we take a look at our self-identity, we find we are fundamentally identified with a constellation of self-images and self-concepts. When we become identified with this constellation of self-concepts, it can be very limiting. There is no judgment in identifying ourselves in this way. It doesn't mean there's something wrong or bad when we are engaged in our personal identity.

One of the fundamental differentiations in Nonviolent Communication is that when we mix our evaluations with our observations, we believe in our thoughts. Someone says or does something in relation to me or someone else that stimulates pain, and my mind says, "This person is mean and inconsiderate." I become identified with that thought and, in other words, I believe that it is true. One of the ways our thinking mind functions is that we take our interpretations to be the truth, rather than looking at what is observed. This is how the interpretive mind takes mediated experiences to be reality.

In my own experience, it's been illuminating to examine and name my belief systems and where they came from. When I can name the beliefs, then at some point I can experience whatever I am encountering more directly, without those thoughts and without those beliefs.

We want to be able to look at our observations and to recognize, "This is what is true." I'm not talking about any absolute truth, but the relative truth—moment by moment—and how our mind interprets it. Our tendency to judge can be very powerful. And even though we might recognize that we are in a judging, reactive state, it can be very challenging to transform it because there is a certain inertia to it that, in my experience, is based on survival.

The purpose of the mind is to perpetuate its own existence. We are familiar with our mind, and in this way, we can see it as our comfort zone. When we are in the defensive, judgmental mode, there is a part of our mind that wants to justify, defend, attack, rebel, attempt to be right, and maintain the status quo. This part of our mind we identify with is attached to the familiar and the known, and it's this part that is uncomfortable with what is unknown.

Stephen Schwartz also addresses the survival aspect of the mind:

The ego mechanism (which I see as the protective and defensive survival structures), seems to be helpful because it pushes down what otherwise would seem to be unutterably painful. Our life here is tragic in this respect. We feel we are separated forever... from mother, father, universe, and must make it without help. And the ego keeps us always in exile. Our true being longs for freedom.[5]

In many spiritual approaches and traditions, this survival tendency of the mind is traditionally called, the "ego." My understanding of the ego, however, is different than this. For me, the ego is not some nasty enemy I have to transcend and get over; it's not an enemy that is keeping me unenlightened and imprisoned in dark places. I see the ego as the part of my system that has developed based on conditioning from my culture and the many painful experiences I've had in my life. The ego serves to protect me from pain and from whatever seems threatening, so I am defended against perceived danger. This protection often looks like an ego-based reaction or defense.

The brain is wired for biological and physical survival. And I want to acknowledge that there's a distinction between physical survival and psychological survival. Somehow, when we perceive an emotional or psychological threat, the biological survival process that exists in the brain as a natural and necessary part of human functioning gets confused and transposes emotional survival into physical survival. This activates reactions that would be helpful in physical survival, but it limits the quality of my experience when my need is emotional safety.

The mind's confusion between physical and psychological survival gives rise to psychological defense mechanisms that keep me emotionally closed and unable to be vulnerable. This can happen because, based on conditioning and past trauma, I carry a core belief that something is a threat to my physical existence. On some level, my being, my consciousness, believes there is a threat to my survival, and I react with the kind of strength and force needed to protect my life.

There is still a lot to be done in the exploration of trauma and how it activates that survival part of the brain, usurps the power of the cognitive mind, and ultimately results in acting from reactivity for survival.

Awareness and Observing

In this work of self-compassion, there is an important and very subtle distinction between observing awareness and the thinking mind. That which we observe "with" is awareness, which you could say is the medium of all our experiencing. What we observe is the content or form of our experience, which includes our thoughts.

One of the things I've discovered is that it is not the mind that observes; it is awareness that observes. One of our primary challenges occurs when we mix up our thoughts with awareness. When we observe something, and we mix it in, or intertwine it, with our thinking about what we observe, this mixture becomes an obstacle to fully experiencing "what is."

Thoughts can be seen as objects of awareness. All other forms of experiencing can also be seen as the objects of awareness. Awareness is what sheds light on the thoughts. We call this the light of awareness. The different forms of experiencing are thinking, emotional feeling, bodily sensation, and the overall thrust of the life force that moves in and through our being. This life force manifests as what matters to us, what we are valuing, and what we are needing. The subtle, formless container of all experiencing is awareness itself.

Presence and Experiencing

There are two primary dimensions in observing and experiencing: the observing awareness and the form or the content of experiencing. These two dimensions are interwoven. I've created a conceptual framework for understanding these two dimensions that I call "Presence and Experiencing." Although these lists are presented side by side, there is no correspondence between the "Presence" list on the left and the "Experiencing" list on the right. The relationship is that "Formless" is the observer and "Form" is that which is observed.

PRESENCE
Formless
Awareness
Witnessing
Noticing
Attention
Attending to
Being With

EXPERIENCING
Form
Thinking, Imagining, and Emotion
Sensation and Sensing *(dense and subtle)*
Longing and Yearning
Valuing and Needing
Acting and Behaving *(includes speaking)*

Presence is formless. Awareness (as well as all the other words listed under "Presence") is an expression of the nature of presence. Awareness, witnessing, noticing, attention, attending to, and being with can be described as qualities of presence. All of these terms are synonymous.

Experiencing has content and form. These include the cognitive dimension of thinking and imagining; the emotional dimension, and the sensation dimension that includes experiencing along a spectrum of dense and subtle sensing; the dimension of the life force that manifests as a longing or yearning of the heart, valuing and needing; and the dimension of observable

113

behaviors of acting (including speaking and listening).

The basic dynamic of inner or self-compassion is cultivating our ability to inhabit observing awareness. As we inhabit this awareness, we establish an intimate relationship between the one who observes and our interior experiencing.

When I become conscious that I am dwelling in the observing awareness, it's not so much that I'm *observing* my awareness but that it is who I am. I've heard the expression countless times before, "I become aware of awareness." But I'm not observing my awareness in that sense. I *am* it. I am dwelling in the observing awareness, and I am resting in it.

This is a little different than the observing awareness that observes the content of my experience. When dwelling in the observing awareness, there is always a form of experiencing. It doesn't matter whether the content is flowing and radiant or obstructive and constricted; I'm observing while experiencing at the same time. It is not one or the other that is happening.

Presence is always recognizing my experience. The more in presence I am, the more there is flow, equanimity, and peace.

Presence and Allowing

Presence is not something I do; it is something I allow. The quality of presence is formless. When I observe presence, I see that it is infinite. It goes beyond me. The thinking mind and the conditioned mind will argue with anything. Presence does not argue. Presence simply allows.

Cultivating inner presence involves an intention and commitment to be watchfully aware, moment by moment. It's important to recognize when I am in the flow of life and when I am not in the flow of life. When I do this, I can recognize experientially that I am sometimes in an unrestricted feeling flow or a contracted state, or maybe I am experiencing a combination of both.

"Am I enjoying myself?" is a helpful inquiry. "What needs are alive or not alive in me right now? What do I choose at this moment?" These inquiries bring a living awareness that reveals to me my needs that are met and unmet and to what extent I am in a life flow. I can then consciously choose to be with the life in me, to mourn or to celebrate, and to take action or not.

This awareness is watchfulness. It is a non-judging but discerning awareness. I want to remain present and alive to the flow of consciousness and living energy as it flows through me, moment by moment. Even in this moment, as you read this, see if you can feel the energy as it moves through your awareness. What are the qualities of this energy? Perhaps the energy of care? Of clarity? Of inspiration?

The Power of Attention

Awareness is attention. The quality of our experience and, therefore, the quality of our lives, is a function of how we pay attention, of how we focus our attention.

Many years ago, at a pivotal point in my own development, I discovered that all practice is the discipline of attention; it is not the form that supports attention. For example, I can do a yoga practice or any number of other practices, but fundamentally, at the heart of any practice is the discipline of attention—which is how I focus my awareness—and the link and connection my attention has to energy or experience. The fundamental core of my practice is seated in my awareness and how I direct my awareness to my experiencing.

The practices I present here are fundamentally a cultivating of my attention and my awareness. Sarah McLean talks about attention in a similar way:

Your attention is powerful, full of power. The kind of attention I am talking about is your non-judgmental, welcoming, loving attention. This attention energizes and enlivens all things in your life. Your attention arises from inside you, from that presence we'll call your "inner self." What you pay attention to and how you pay attention is how you use your power. When you reclaim your attention, you reclaim your power, your true power and this leads to a peaceful and more fulfilling and creative life.[7]

Sarah's words communicate an essential aspect of the cultivation, development, and practice of cultivating presence through the transformational, spiritual practices such as self-compassion.

PRACTICE: Guided Meditation on Awareness

You might want to record the following meditation first and then play it to guide you.

Note that the "…pause…" is an invitation to give yourself time to notice and be with whatever is present.

Let's begin:

I invite you to close your eyes, settle, and get comfortable in your seat, sitting as straight as you can.

…pause…

Bring attention to your body and to your breath. Simply acknowledge your awareness. Breathe and rest your awareness. Notice that your awareness surrounds and imbues all that you are experiencing.

…pause…

Whatever arises in your experience, simply be aware of it. Thinking, images. emotional feelings, bodily sensing, and longing are always in movement, they flow and change.

119

…pause…

Awareness is unmoving. It is always here as a presence, encompassing, embracing, unmoving, outside of time and space. Refrain from trying to understand this with your mind. I invite you to notice as much as you can. There is such an intimate, intertwined, co-arising of awareness itself and all the forms of your experiencing. Awareness is always present even when you don't notice it.

…pause…

As you rest in your awareness, embracing and allowing the flow of all your experience without resisting it, find your strength, your power, and your equanimity. Feel your aliveness…

…pause…

Whenever you are ready, slowly move your attention back into the space where you are. Allow yourself to take a deeper breath and then open your eyes. I encourage you to journal your experience.

Cultivating the Compassionate Observer

I want to unpack the fundamental practice of self-compassion using this diagram I refer to as "The Life Process in Reaction". It is impossible to create a structure that replicates an internal, subjective experience, but this is my attempt to do that. The whole outer circle represents the interior experience. The outer circle is what I would call the awareness and our essential being. This is the place of observing. Descriptions of the content of our experience are in the middle circle. When we practice observing, we are cultivating the one who observes experience compassionately, allowing transformation to take place so we can reach the life energy underneath the content of our reactivity.

At the top of the diagram is an image of a cloud that represents a life event or stimulus occurring at any given time in our life. This life event is something we receive and the circle underneath the cloud represents the container or medium in which we take in life. The stimulus enters through our essential being and our awareness. The amount of spaciousness we have depends on our level of awareness and to what extent we are identified with reactive experiencing. The more I practice bringing compassion to my reaction, the more I notice my space of awareness grows, my center of gravity is strengthened, and my essential being or true self increasingly becomes my predominant state of being.

The center of the diagram represents the content of experiencing in a reactive state. This takes the forms of reactive thinking, reactive feelings, and contractive bodily sensations.

The words on the left side of the cloud describe the primary elements of this self-compassion

The Life Process in Reaction

Cultivating the One Who Compassionately Observes

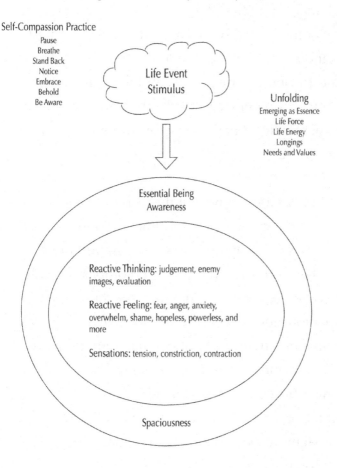

Self-Compassion Practice
Pause
Breathe
Stand Back
Notice
Embrace
Behold
Be Aware

Life Event
Stimulus

Unfolding
Emerging as Essence
Life Force
Life Energy
Longings
Needs and Values

Essential Being
Awareness

Reactive Thinking: judgement, enemy
images, evaluation

Reactive Feeling: fear, anger, anxiety,
overwhelm, shame, hopeless, powerless, and
more

Sensations: tension, constriction, contraction

Spaciousness

practice, which is simply a practice of inner noticing and inner embracing. I always want to remember to pause first and breathe. Breathing changes the physiology of reactivity into a more receptive state. Then, metaphorically, I want to stand back because a little space is required for me to observe myself. I can then remember to notice, embrace, and behold whatever experiencing I have in my awareness. I want to be aware.

What we are cultivating through our practice of self-compassion is "the one who compassionately observes." The more I am able to dwell in awareness, notice compassionately, and embrace my internal reaction with a spaciousness that allows it to give rise to the transformative effects of compassion, the more I develop the center of gravity within myself of the one who compassionately observes. The more I practice this, the more I have available the capacity to be present and compassionate with my own inner experiencing and with others as I receive them.

The words on the right side of the cloud describe what unfolds in spacious awareness. As I cultivate the compassionate observer within me, my true essence emerges. I become more in touch with my life force and life energy. I experience this as the fullness of my longings and in the forms of my needs and values. Through this compassionate practice, my life force becomes increasingly available to me.

One of the reasons I use a variety of words for the same experience is that different words connote different meanings for people. Consider the words "witnessing," "observing," and "noticing." For me, the experience is the same for all of these, only the words are different.

If I "behold" something, this means there is something in front of me. I notice it is there, it is alive, and it is real. I take it all in, I behold it. When I am beholding fully, there is no part of my attention that is elsewhere. For example, if I am in a museum and I see a work of art that my mind would evaluate as incredible and inspiring, I would stand in front of this artwork and breathe...and experience awe as I behold this piece of art. This experience of beholding is a kind of cherishing, where I allow all of my attention to be there, present to the art.

When we think of embracing, many of us may think of hugging something or someone. What I mean in this diagram is a more subtle kind of embracing. As I behold something, I am embracing it with my full awareness, with my full heart. There's an intimacy between me and the object that I am beholding. I am close to it. I embrace it with gentleness, with kindness, with inclusion. For me, there is no distinction between beholding and embracing. These are simply metaphors because experience itself goes beyond the physicality where metaphors reside.

Restoring Wholeness

If I have an experience in which I am triggered and pain is stimulated, first, I want to acknowledge that I am experiencing a state of contraction. That acknowledgment is an important form of observing awareness. I've begun the self-compassion process.

Everything I do internally, anything I focus my awareness on, is in relationship to the reactivated state I've just acknowledged. I breathe. My first intention is to allow whatever is arising in me to be just as it is. I notice that judgments are there. I recognize them. The reactive contraction of my feelings—such as fear, anger, and overwhelm—are there. I recognize them. Sensations are there. I recognize them.

It may take a bit of time just to focus my attention on this inner process. And bringing my awareness to the thoughts, feelings, and sensations happens before I connect to the life force, to my longings. But I remember that at the very heart of this reactive state is the life force itself, the beauty of my unmet needs.

By directing my consciousness and focusing my awareness on my internal experiencing, I am cultivating and developing this observing awareness. Now, my reactive state may not transform immediately, but when I reside in the observing awareness, that, in and of itself, begins to yield the transformational process. It unfolds.

For example, when I stay with and compassionately embrace my reactive feeling of anger, it will always unfold into fear. It may start as a frozen fear, but if I can stay with it, a softening occurs, and gradually there is a relaxing into what I describe as a vulnerable fear. In the fear experience, there may be other painful emotions that I want to notice, allow, and embrace. At the heart of these emotions is always a link to my needs. When I can connect bodily to the energy of my needs, this embodied fullness, for me, is the beginning of the restoration of my wholeness.

PRACTICE: Noticing—A Solo or Paired Process

This practice cultivates our ability to just "notice," which is an element of our awareness. It is an invitation to be aware of experiencing itself, whatever thoughts, images, feelings, sensations, or longings are there.

Take a moment to step back and notice whatever you can of your internal experiencing. Now notice that you are being aware of that.

If you are doing this practice alone, it can be helpful to use a journal to note down your responses to the prompts. If you are processing with a partner, you can share your responses aloud.

Let's begin:

I invite you to bring your attention to your body and to your breath. Relax and breathe.

…pause…

Now, focus your attention on your present moment experiencing, whatever it is. If it's a stimulated, triggered state, then so be it. Notice whatever you are experiencing.

…pause…

As you pay attention to what you are experiencing right now, notice and identify any thoughts, images, or stories. Journal or share this aloud with your partner.

…pause…

Notice and identify any emotional feelings. What are you feeling now? Notice if what you are feeling changes as you pay attention to it. Then journal or share aloud with your partner.

…pause…

Notice and identify sensations. Take your time; there's no rush. Feel whatever you are sensing and journal or share this with your partner.

…pause…

Notice, acknowledge, and identify whatever is alive in you in terms of your needs, your longings, what you value, what matters to you at this moment in your life. Journal or share this aloud.

…pause…

Now notice your awareness that contains all of your experiencing. "Step back" and sense the content of your awareness, even as it moves and changes its shape. Notice the content of all your experience…all your thoughts, the whole constellation of feelings, sensations, and the energy of your needs. This is the most subtle step. You are noticing all your experience and then recognizing and witnessing that it is awareness that contains your experiencing.

…pause…

Now bring your attention back to the content of your experiencing. You are simply moving your attention back and forth between awareness that is noticing and the forms of experiencing being noticed. If you can, notice the interfusion of the observing awareness and the form of experiencing (thoughts, feelings, sensations, and longings). This is a subtle process...moving back and forth or even simultaneously.

...pause...

Complete this practice by sharing with your partner or journaling for yourself whatever is arising in you.

Owning Our Experience

I've found that noticing what I am doing in relation to pain, particularly if I am projecting or my reaction comes from a defensive or protective part of me, is an essential part of taking ownership of my inner experience. Taking ownership can mean that when I feel pain in relation to a stimulus, I notice there is a thought in me and that this thought is a story. I may not say this thought to the person. I would prefer to acknowledge it first with myself—inwardly, interiorly—before I speak.

Taking ownership is the recognition and the conscious acknowledgment that what is arising is coming out of my own interior space, my own system, and my own history. An important support in loosening my fusion with my reaction is to name whatever I can notice in my awareness. By naming it, I might be able to feel it. Can I feel the sensation without bouncing off its energy by either attacking or withdrawing?

For example, let's imagine I am having a conversation with someone, and I say something that is important to me, but the response I get tells me that my intention has not been received. I then interpret the other person's response as an evaluation of what I said. I'm evaluating their evaluation. When I receive their response in this way, I may first feel frustrated or angry. My mind says, *"Why aren't they getting what I said? I thought I was being pretty clear."*

If I can take enough time to just stay with my thoughts, I find that almost always underneath them, I feel a sense of tenderness. I notice a part of me that feels scared. Almost always, this part of me has a legacy of the pain that the little boy in me felt when he wasn't seen or heard. When I am able to feel this, I may touch the natural pain of grief. As I stay tender with this naturally arising pain, it links me to what really matters to me, and I begin to feel the energy of acceptance. Even though the need for acceptance was not met in the original conversation, I can now experience the energy of my longing for acceptance and being seen. It is this energy that restores me.

Differentiated Unity

In the course of living, there is a continual dance between the exterior of life and how we receive and experience it with the interior impressions. These interior, energetic impressions contain living information. How we attend to these impressions is the fundamental focus of this spiritual work of Living Compassion. Another way to express this is through the commonly-voiced adage, *"It's not what happens to you; it's what you do with what happens to you."* It is relatively easy to intellectually understand that our perspective affects our experience, and it can be an additional challenge to know it experientially. In a disconnected experiencing, we mix in our evaluations, our judgments, and our reactions about what happens to us and what we observe. It is this reactive thinking that creates our disconnection, distress, and suffering. These two dimensions, observing awareness and content of experiencing, are so inextricably intertwined that it's a challenge to experience the distinction between them. The interfusion between them is so subtle; I cannot experience something without being aware of it. It requires a considerable amount of practice and skill to develop the clarity of what can be called a "differentiated unity." When we can experience this differentiated unity with awareness and experiencing, the function of our mind becomes creative, becomes inspirational because it is seated in the essential consciousness of the heart itself.

When I am in an unobstructed state of being—observing and experiencing the content at the same time—there is a wholeness with the differentiation within that unity. This is not duality, it is differentiation. One meaning of the word "duality" is that there is a kind of polarization: good and bad, right and wrong. That is different from the recognition of a unity that is differentiated.

When I am engaged in witnessing my observing awareness in relation to what I am experiencing, the quality of my experience is enhanced, enriched, and made fuller. There is more flow as I do this. It does affect the quality of my experiencing.

Developing Capacity

People sometimes ask if it is possible to reside permanently in a vulnerable, undefended state. I, personally, don't reside in that state permanently, but I think it is possible. But living in an undefended, and therefore authentic state permanently isn't the main point of what we are doing with these spiritual practices.

Our work here has to do with the concept of development. I'll use an analogy of physical exercise to illustrate this. If I am fifty pounds heavier than my ideal weight and I want to be fit, I work on my diet and my exercise, and I become more fit. Now, developing the physical body is different from the movements in our psychological states, but there is a degree of similarity with improving well-being through

137

exercise and diet. To sustain what could be called the "valued" state, I maintain my diet and exercise practice. If I let go of that practice, then I'm going to slide back into the previous state.

The state of consciousness can be seen as a psychological state. It is a developmental process in which the more I practice, the more my center of gravity begins to strengthen and transform my being into the flow of life, residing in my heart in non-reactive, undefended wholeness.

Maintaining and sustaining a practice is required to shift the center of my gravity from one predominantly identified in the reactive state to one more and more able to hold presence with self.

I've discovered through practice that there is a certain state we shift into that I call a preponderance state over the others. With a dedicated and committed practice, we can shift into living preponderantly in our wholeness.

When this happens, it doesn't mean we don't shift back into other states, but the more I practice, the more I find myself dwelling in fullness and wholeness.

I remember being asked, "Do you get triggered anymore?" That's easy to answer. "Of course I do!" But over time I've noticed that there are three characteristics of how this shift toward fullness and wholeness manifests. First, the frequency of being triggered is reduced. Second, the intensity of my reaction is much less, and I don't get lost in it as much as I did in the past. And third, the duration of my triggered state is significantly less.

I think it is beneficial to see the development of wholeness as something we practice, not as a means to a goal of residing in some permanent state. As I've mentioned earlier, seeking any specific outcome has the drawback of coming from deficiency, the orientation exemplified by "I'm not there yet" thinking.

Two-Minute Self-Empathy

My capacity to be empathic with someone is founded on my ability to connect with myself. When I receive a reaction from another person, I first want to take time to sit with myself and identify specifically what this person said. I want to bring my attention to my inner reaction, to open to it and allow it, to let myself feel any pain or anything else I may be feeling. I want to transform my judgments, to be aware of bodily sensations, and to connect to the longings and needs that are not being fulfilled in this interaction.

Staying with the pain of our reactions can be hard, and that is one of the reasons I'm offering these practices. If you find that it is hard, it would be valuable to pay attention to that and to ask yourself, "What are the first moments in my experience of inner compassion that are difficult, and what am I telling myself? That I'm not able to do it?" Identify and remember those first moments; they can give you a clue about what you can do.

Maybe you will realize that in this interaction that triggered your reaction, you are not capable of being empathic at this time. Can you stand back and see what thoughts you are telling yourself?

This is an initial step of self-compassion, and it takes place in your own space. You are not in the relational space because you are not able to access your resources for empathy. A principle I learned many years ago in NVC is that I can't offer empathy if I'm in pain or if I'm triggered. I don't have the resources. I have to restore myself through self-empathy or through receiving it from someone else before I can offer empathy to another.

PRACTICE: Simple Remembering

In the midst of everyday life, even in the midst of doing, just pause for two minutes…that is all, just two minutes.

Take those minutes to stop and notice what you are feeling.

Pause, notice your body, and name what you sense.

Notice what you are feeling emotionally.

Notice what you are telling yourself.

That's all. It's a simple practice.

I'm not saying it is easy. I think it takes a commitment to give yourself two or three minutes to pause...simply notice...and ask yourself, *"What am I feeling and needing?"*

Living Free

I would characterize my life practice as a continual, embodied mindfulness. I'm not bopping along in my life...doing okay...then I get triggered, and I say to myself, *"Okay, now it's time to practice self-compassion."* That is not how I experience a spiritual life practice.

Living Compassion is my continual, embodied mindfulness practice because the longing in my being is to live and feel the fullness every moment of my life. The continual sense of intimacy with the life in me is a way of living. As Lawrence Heller has said, *"The price of freedom is eternal mindfulness."*[8] I want to live mindful, aware, and free at every moment.

Chapter 5

Can we see directly into what our experience is without trying to modify it, improve it, change it, condition it, without searching for the pleasure, pushing away the pain? We constantly generate descriptions by which we live. We know that life is not contained within the conceptual realm; it is not described accurately by those ideas, yet we live in relationship to those ideas.

At every moment we have the capacity to fall back into the defended space of the known and we have the ability to abandon the moment and enter into the unknown of what is next. Let us face the full range of the human potential by engaging the fear of a negative expression and the attraction of a positive expression, both of which are terrifying. We are as afraid of our love as we are of our anger. The expression of the unknown is a deep feeling… not feeling in terms of emotion, which is also conditioned just like thought is, but feeling that is the totality of the energetic movement in the system expressing itself through some aspect. This is a radical life. While it is fresh and alive, it may be totally unrecognizable to us to be completely authentic in the moment.

~ Steven Harrison[9]

Fundamental to this process we call Nonviolent Communication and this body of work I call Living Compassion, is our relationship to what arises within us as we receive life. This quality of our relationship is dependent on how we meet life's energies as we receive them in all their forms, whether these energies come from other people or our own choices about what we do and say. We are cultivating our capacities to embrace these energies with compassion as they occur in the ever-changing landscape of our inner lives.

Impermanence

The nature of life is ever-changing. We understand this conceptually when we observe life, and we see that it is always changing. In fact, everything changes. Some things change at a faster pace than others. Things change in the exterior world, and our interior experiencing is also always changing and moving.

Related to this worldview is a Buddhist concept known as impermanence. Living with impermanence means living with the understanding and the acceptance that everything changes; everything comes and goes. It means living in the awareness that everything flows, everything is constantly moving and changing in our inner and outer lives.

To stay in the present moment, living in and from our center, requires accepting and not resisting change as it occurs. That is easy to say and perhaps conceptually easy to understand, and it is another thing altogether to experience. I like what Alan Watts says about the inevitability of change and the discomfort that arises with it, *"The only way to make sense out of change is to plunge into it, to move with it, and to join the dance."*[10] I invite you to notice within yourself the nature of change and how you meet it.

Embracing Life or Resisting Life

What is the significance of accepting that which I experience, whether it's something I enjoy or something I find uncomfortable? The more I grow in my capacity to live with impermanence, the more I am able to embrace my unmet needs. This means being comfortable with discomfort, with what is unwanted. Henry Wadsworth Longfellow put this simply, *"For after all, the best thing one can do when it is raining is to let it rain."*[11] Resistance is like railing against the rain, trying to move the stream of life in the opposite direction. I want to notice any resistance and become curious about the part of me that is resisting. I notice that in my mind, the part of me that resists is holding on to what is familiar and known.

Relationships change. We grow apart, we lose connections. We come together, we reestablish trust, and we strengthen our connections. Accepting change is accepting outer circumstances and accepting the inner experience of what is unexpected or unwanted.

One of the ways I know I am resisting instead of accepting change is that there's a part of me that wants to manage and control what is occurring or what is arising within me, I want to fix it, and to make it better. This response comes from the energy of resistance.

When I experience something unpleasant or uncomfortable, what follows is either the unobstructed natural pain as the situation arises, or I resist the experience of pain and then I suffer. When I am in the suffering state, what I am resisting on one level is the flow of life. To be open to a life experience is to feel it in an

149

undefended way, and that requires my vulnerability. This is what I mean when I say, "I'm not resisting."

As John Green said, *"When you stopped wishing things wouldn't fall apart, you'd stop suffering when they did."*[12] This seems to be part of the human condition. When things fall apart and don't go the way we want them to go, this brings up our suffering, mostly because we have not yet developed the capacity to be with and embrace the experience we call pain.

Acceptance Is Not Resignation

This work of creating a space of compassion is founded on accepting and welcoming what is, both in the exterior world and as it arises within us. When I talk about accepting, I'm not talking about agreeing with anything or anyone. If something happens or someone says something I am uncomfortable with, when I accept it, this doesn't signify that I agree with or condone what was said or done. I am not saying, *"It's okay."* If I condone something, this could lead to an experience of resignation, which is a misinterpretation of what I mean by acceptance.

So, when I accept something, this doesn't mean I am resigned to it. Resignation feels and sounds like giving up: *"Oh, what's the use? I might as well accept it, there's nothing I can do about it anyway. The situation is hopeless."* When I am resigned or I condone something, I feel a particular quality of energy in my body—a sinking down, a sense of giving up—that restricts the flow of life as it moves through me. This energy affects my experience of openness, and instead of resonance, I feel a dissonance within.

When I am accepting or allowing something, I want to ask myself, *"What is it I am letting go of?"* One of the things I let go of when I am in acceptance is the tendency to try to manage and control.

Accepting is an invitation to feel what is present without resisting it. I allow myself to feel the energy and intensity of my experience. When I do this, I am cultivating more room inside of myself and in my capacity to feel energy, to feel life. I am welcoming life.

Freedom with Discomfort

I've discovered that if I want to be in an inner state of freedom with respect to all the experiences of life, then I must learn how to embrace discomfort. I want to learn how to allow and to feel the intensity of sensation that is at the heart of anything uncomfortable. To do this, I just stay with my inner experiencing. I don't push myself into the experience of pain, but gently stay with it.

When I am able to stay with the intensity at the core of discomfort, what is likely to happen in my system is that a profound inner part of me says, *"No! Don't go there!"* This part comes from my history and conditioning, and it learned how to protect and defend me from feeling anything that was uncomfortable. Cultivating our capacity to tolerate discomfort relaxes our fears and grows our inner freedom to embrace more of life.

Whenever there's an intensity, what it shows me is that something really matters to me; there is something that I care about. Intensity shows me what the value is in what matters to me. I have the choice to look beneath the discomfort or to let my mind take over and resist it while judging myself (or other people) or feeling overwhelmed. There's a choice point here. The experience of intensity is life speaking to me, it is the energy of my needs speaking to me. Can I connect to life? As much as I can, I want to stay in tune with the energy of this intensity that is taking me to what I am needing and valuing.

If I stay in the intensity of an experience to the limit of my capacity to tolerate it, I remember I can back off. I can breathe. I can remember that there is no urgency, even though the intensity of the pain might be pushing me toward immediate release. I want to remember and recognize these compassion practices: *"I can be patient, I don't need to push myself,"* and *"I can breathe."*

At every moment, I want to be as present, relaxed, and open as I am able to be. Whenever I am not able to be in this state, I want to be with that inability. I let myself feel the discomfort and resistance to my limited capacity, with as much openness and care as I bring to all the elements of my experience.

Physical Survival or Emotional Pain

Emotional pain, in NVC terms, arises when something happens that surrounds something we care about in which our needs aren't met. Given our conditioning, embracing pain is seemingly counterintuitive. Our mind might even see the concept of embracing pain as masochistic: "What do you mean enjoy pain?" So, turning toward pain is a radical approach to our conditioning and to the survival mechanisms embedded in us from the culture and our training that tell us to make pain go away and to hang onto pleasure.

From the aspects of physical survival and physical well-being, within the natural order of things, there is something life-serving about resistance to pain. We don't want to perpetuate the pain if we can support ourselves in our well-being. But this tendency starts to reinforce itself in very deep, unconscious, and habitual ways when physical pain translates into emotional and psychological pain. We then develop a view of ourselves and of life, that we are not able to tolerate the intensity of discomfort.

At the heart of much of my emotional pain, my psychological pain, is the need to feel safe and secure, which usually means some kind of comfort with the familiar and the known.

I want to make the distinction between physical pain and emotional pain. When I engage in a practice, I am simply allowing myself to be with it and to notice whatever is alive, even physical pain. My experience is that physical pain can also have an emotional component that adds to how distressing the experience can be.

When I have emotional resistance to physical pain, it is this that creates my suffering, rather than the physical pain being the suffering itself. Emotional resistance might sound like, *"Oh, my God! What is this?! Why won't it go away? Now I'm miserable! I can't do what I wanted to do!"* These kinds of thoughts can go on and on and on. When I take a moment to stay with the experience of physical pain before I act automatically, I find that I can create a space in which I do not emotionally resist the physical pain. This space affects my experience of physical pain.

Befriending Myself

Experiencing life, I am engaging in life: hearing it, receiving it, and participating in it. When I tune into life energy on a felt, energetic level, I am paying attention to it. By paying attention to the life force, I am more likely to be able to stay in the flow of this energy rather than resist it. I don't have any control over the existence of life force. It is just here. What I do have a choice over is how I meet the life force.

This energy of life, this force of life, manifests through us and throughout all of life. So, the choice is either to go on with my conditioning to obstruct it, which is usually unconscious and habituated, or to develop my capacity to live in flow. I can do this by slowly, gently, and compassionately recognizing those felt obstructions and simply allowing them. Life shows me over and over again that at the heart of those obstructions is precious life reaching for life.

I want to remember the principle that whenever I am experiencing pain, it is because of my precious unmet need. I want to know this not only cognitively, but also to feel it. As I develop this capacity for self-compassion, I begin to notice when I feel something uncomfortable (a restriction, something that I don't enjoy), and I start to move towards it with trust. I become curious. I am aware I have a choice.

Gradually and with practice, as I move towards pain, I realize that it is not the inner enemy. The pain is not a "bad" part of me trying to make my life miserable. It is simply an aspect of me. Increasingly, as I learn how to approach my inner pain, I begin to be compassionate with those parts of myself that I previously ran away from when I didn't have the capacity to be with and feel my pain. I begin to befriend myself. This is a form of self-love. I am developing an intimate relationship with myself.

I find using inquiries helpful for inviting clarity and connection with myself. A couple of inquiries that have helped me with self-compassion are:

How can I be in an intimate nonviolent, compassionate relationship with someone else unless I am able to be compassionate and nonviolent with all parts of myself? How can I be with somebody without pushing them away if I can't be with myself without pushing parts of myself away?

Love is attention. Love is awareness: nonjudgmental, accepting, allowing awareness. Love is a component of compassion. Like love, compassion is infinitely patient. It doesn't push me into anything. It allows.

Questioning Motivation

I want to be aware if I am avoiding something out of fear or if I am moving towards something from a space of self-connection. There's no right or wrong way. I want to be conscious of the motivation that is moving me towards whatever choice or strategy I am making.

For me, if I am moving towards something, the motivating energy is always care. If I am moving away from something, then the motivating energy is always fear. If the energy is fear, I want to notice it. The fear is inviting me. It is calling me. It is needing and wanting compassion. This process is an invitation to feel life.

If I am fearful, I want to allow myself to feel fearful, to let myself connect with it. I ask myself: *"What is the part of me that is afraid?"* For example, it may be that I am not fully trusting that I will be able to maintain my center and my presence when I hear this other person speak to me. I'm not confident they are going to communicate with me in a way that is fully considerate and respectful of me and in which I will be seen.

I want to transform my fear as much as I can with self-empathy because this will help me to move towards what I care about, what I am valuing and needing. Fear is often connected with a need for safety. I want to examine what I am telling myself. What thoughts and beliefs do I have about what I think is safety and security? This has been important for me to explore as an inquiry within myself. The more I do this, the more I find this source of safety and security is already within me. I don't let go of that. I let go of the externally referenced need that I can only feel safe if something in my environment is a certain way.

It feels so good to move towards something, towards self-care. When I'm taking care of myself, I feel empowered. I have found this practice is especially important in situations where my choices seem limited.

Grief and Beauty

The experience of self-compassion is one in which I allow. I actually let in and become vulnerable to that which previously was intolerable. I let in the information from life without judging it, without interpreting it. In the

161

quotation at the beginning of this chapter, Steven Harrison asks: *"Can we see directly into what our experience is without trying to modify it, improve it, change it, or condition it?"* I want to be able to see and face what's going on in life and in the world. I want to be able to let it in. When I am able to let in all of life, it touches my heart and breaks my heart open.

Allowing myself to feel the natural grief or pain that can result from feeling something that was previously intolerable is living with a broken-open heart. Opening myself to feel this grief vulnerably is to face it with my heart and with my body. This kind of pain is a natural feeling, a sacred feeling. The practice of grief and mourning is essential to maintaining and dwelling in the flow of my life.

Mourning is a celebration of the aliveness within my sadness. It is a practice that moves me towards equanimity, a consciousness without preference for one feeling experience over another. When I am in this state of equanimity, I am connected to the aliveness at the heart of both happiness and sadness.

Moving toward pain and feeling grief is not an easy practice for most of us, and sometimes it gets very difficult for me, too. When this happens, I make a deliberate effort to spend time with myself or to receive support in the loving presence of another person. The more I allow myself to feel intensity, the more I am able to be with the fullness of the energy within any situation in life. When I can be with the fullness, I am brought in touch with the beauty of life in the pain. In touch with this beauty, I become a vehicle for spirit and life rather than an obstruction to it.

PRACTICE: Exploring My Inner Experience

These questions are offered as inquiries for inner exploration. Each question is an invitation to connect to what arises in you as you receive it. Allow yourself to explore your inner experiencing in response to the question rather than trying to answer the question definitively.

If you are doing this practice alone, you might want to record the questions first and then play your recording, pausing to receive and then respond to each one. You may want to use a journal to note your responses to the questions.

If you are processing with another person, your partner can ask the questions and then wait as a silent witness while you share your responses aloud to each question.

Don't rush through this practice. Wherever it says, "…pause…," this is an invitation to take the time you need to connect with each question so you can fully receive it. Connect to what's alive and then share (perhaps write) what arises.

Let's begin:

I invite you to bring your attention to your body and to your breath. Relax and breathe.

…pause…

Now, regarding your whole life, how do you resist your experience of life?

…pause…

In your relationships, what kind of expectations do you have of others and of life?

…pause…

How are you attached to outcome?

…pause…

How do you hold onto pleasure and avoid painful experiences?

…pause…

Can you sense the possibility of welcoming discomfort?

…pause…

Can you imagine embracing and feeling okay with the unexpected?

…pause…

Can you welcome the uncertainty of what is to come?

…pause…

Can you imagine being at peace with insecurity?

…pause…

Can you open yourself to embracing the next moment?

…pause…

Can you sense the possibility of welcoming what is unwanted?

…pause…

Can you imagine growing in your capacity to embrace unmet needs?

…pause…

Can you let go of your need for safety and security?

…pause…

Can you open to the possibility of relaxing your avoidance of pain?

…pause…

Can you rest into trust in yourself?

…pause…

Can you rest into trusting life?

…pause…

Wherever you finish in this process, end with this invitation: *"Relaxing into the center of your being, breathe and feel."*

There is a simplicity in mystery that simply says, "I don't know." And when I say, "I don't know," a spaciousness arises within me and in the relational field between me and another.

CHAPTER 6

It is only through letting our heart break that we discover something unexpected: The heart cannot actually break, it can only break open. To live with a broken-open heart is to experience life full strength. When the heart breaks open, it marks the beginning of a real love affair with this world. It is a broken-hearted love affair, rather than the conventional kind based on hope and expectation. Only in this fearless love that can respond to life's pain as well as its beauty can we be of real help to ourselves or anyone else in this difficult age.

~ John Welwood[12]

Living with my heart open, for me, means living from my vulnerability and a willingness to engage all the experiences of life as fully as I can. To the extent I can live in this openhearted way, I am living in a flow of energetic movement, of coming and going.

John Welwood's words point to what I call *living in the heart of gratitude and grief*. Gratitude and grief are not opposites, they are a spectrum (I'm using the term grief synonymously with mourning). As I receive life in any moment, it can bring me the fullness of something I am grateful for, something that nurtures my heart, something wonderful or beautiful that I can take in and that links me to my heart. And, at the very next moment, I can experience something I do not enjoy, something that stimulates pain or difficulty or grief in me. If I want to remain with my heart open, I must be able to receive whatever is difficult for me to experience with a *broken-open* heart.

Living with an open heart brings a particular challenge. So much of our culture and social conditioning have taught us to protect ourselves from emotional pain, to keep our hearts from breaking open. However, to receive an experience in an undefended, open way, I must be vulnerable to it. When I am vulnerable to the pain of an unmet need, what arises in me is natural pain, which is often natural grief or mourning. When I experience natural pain, it is not a contracted experience or one in which I am in a suffering state.

Natural pain links me to my heart. The pain itself reminds me that something matters to me, something is dear to me, something is precious to me. It invites me—even if I can't do this immediately—to be vulnerable and to open myself to this natural ache I feel when I experience a dissonance with something I deeply value. I believe that opening to mourning is an essential part of a spiritual practice. This is living with a broken-open heart.

Celebrating Life

Mourning is a celebration of the aliveness within my sadness and my happiness. It's a practice that moves me towards equanimity, a consciousness without preference for one state over another. This principle is essentially very simple but profound as it calls us into an ongoing practice of living with an open heart: *I want to meet life equally, no matter what it is.* I always aspire to practice this principle, even if I can't do it at every moment.

I want to remain awake because otherwise, I fall into a kind of unconscious, automatic trance of not being as present as I enjoy being. In the midst of the ever-moving, ever-changing flow of life, I want to stop and savor a moment, whether I am experiencing enjoyment, gratitude, or an energy of pain. When what I am experiencing is discomfort, the principle I want to remember over and over again is that pain is an energy that links me to something that matters to me. I don't feel emotional or psychological pain about something that doesn't matter to me, that I don't value.

The nature of this work of Living Compassion is to celebrate through gratitude when something in life nurtures me and opens my heart in joy, peace, fun, love, or whatever the quality is. And I also want to invite my heart to be open with challenging experiences. When I am able to do this, I can celebrate the life within the mourning, and I can stay in a flow so that even when I feel grief, I feel aliveness.

Gratitude and Grief: A 2-Part Process

I use the term "precious" to describe something that is dear to me, something I deeply value. It is a word I often use in my gratitude and mourning practices. Stating what is precious to me in any moment helps me to move intentionally into an open-hearted relationship with life. If there is something I value in the exterior world, I want to name it consciously. If I feel gratitude, I want to go deeper, to take my time to explore my experience of it, and to identify what is precious to me.

A gratitude practice can be a mindful, moment-by-moment exploration. I can deliberately choose one moment and identify what I enjoy in my exterior life. For example, I pause and notice something in the natural world, perhaps the quiet breeze, the sun shining, a beautiful environment. Or maybe I notice some animal I enjoy or a person who has said or done something that touched me. Whatever it is, I slow down and say to myself, *"This is precious to me,"* as I receive it inwardly in my body.

When I experience interiorly what is exteriorly precious *to* me, what is awakened is something precious *in* me. This is experienced as a feeling, an energy, a quality that is felt in my body, in my heart. I feel the physical sensation of it, and it has a beauty and a radiance. When I feel the external beauty as it resides in the internal beauty, it occurs to me that it is the beauty of my heart that can recognize the beauty that's in the world. I want to remember these two different elements of life experience: the exterior *to* me and the interior *in* me. These are the two parts of my approach to gratitude and mourning.

Saying, "This is precious *in* me," connects me with the quality of a need or value that I sense as an energy. For example, if the need is enjoyment, I may experience a quality of warmth, or a quality of peaceful, quiet, joy, or there may be a sense of exhilaration that comes from humor that is mixed with enjoyment. Whatever the energy is, I take it in. I feel the physical sensations in my body.

When I examine my interior experience of "preciousness"— and this is likely to be a different bodily experience each time—several aspects become clear. There is an emotional quality I feel, a resonance. There is an interbeing that happens in my relationship to all of life. And as I recognize and let in what is precious *to* me, what is precious *in* me awakens the beauty and radiance I feel in my body. I experience this as being fed by life. It is a nurturing that feeds my soul.

Liberating the Energy in Suffering

There are many obstacles to experiencing grief and also to experiencing gratitude. If I close myself off from feeling pain, I also close myself off from feeling joy. Both pain and joy require open-heartedness and vulnerability.

One of the things that makes it difficult to experience pain is that most of us have an orientation towards it as something negative. Of course, this attitude is learned. It comes from what we've learned through our own life experiences and from the cultural messages that reinforce the orientation that "pain is bad, and pleasure is good." So we gravitate towards pleasure, hang onto it, grasp it, and have a hard time letting it go when there is a natural change. We experience some pain, and we want to avoid it, we push it away, we try to manage and control it.

My suffering is a function of the stories I tell myself, whether I consciously recognize them or not. My narratives are the source of my suffering, and they are created by thoughts that are usually unconscious and automatic such as, *"It shouldn't be this way!"* or *"Why can't it be easy?"* or other variations of these. When I am identified and fused with this kind of thinking, it becomes beliefs through which I filter life. When I am fused with this kind of thinking, one way to look at it is that I'm not fully in life. I'm separated, as though I'm floating above life in this mental sphere that is only allowing me a limited range of experience.

When I experience the pain and suffering of contraction and reactive thinking, I want to remember that this is an opportunity, that there is an opening, and that this is actually the way to beauty. However, it may not necessarily be easy to remember this because it's easy to get lost and collapse into what the mind calls horrible, horrific, terrible, unacceptable. The practice of compassion draws me to remember always that there is another possibility: that compassion liberates the energy caught in suffering.

Embracing Grief

When there is something that stimulates pain in me, I want to recognize what happens automatically within my consciousness. Can I notice that I'm shying away from my discomfort? Do I notice if I am projecting my pain onto the environment or the other person? Am I judging them with my expectations or my disappointments?

Being with grief is a practice of self-compassion or inner compassion. It is oriented towards a particular way of being with life when it takes the form of grief. So, as in all of my self-compassion practices, the first thing I want to do is to pause and then bring my consciousness to the pain I am experiencing. I want to have an intention to approach the pain with awareness rather than to move away from it.

The practice of inner compassion is one of noticing and allowing whatever pain or grief arises to be there. I give that contracted experience space, and this begins the process.

The pain or grief starts unfolding, so what is underneath it eventually reveals itself. Maybe more pain or grief is revealed. Perhaps reactive feelings surface or the protective, defensive part of the mind is triggered, and there is reactive thinking. As the process unfolds, I name and acknowledge whatever I notice. It may take time to stay with my experience and process this.

Besides pausing and creating a spacious presence within myself, what this grief practice requires is connecting with a caring attention. This tender attention will help me notice if I am moving away from this experience. Everything in my history has taught me that I should do anything other than stay with grief or any other form of pain. However, the more I practice turning toward the pain with tenderness, curiosity, and awareness, the more I can become familiar with the patterned tendencies of how I experience life, how I avoid it, and how I attempt to grasp it.

When I can touch the preciousness of what I am grieving, there is a healing that takes place within me. I may still feel the tenderness of the pain, but it is an open-hearted grief that touches the beauty within the unfulfilled need. If I'm not touching the beauty in my experience, I'm not fully grieving. I'm not in my experience in the fullness of the grief. That doesn't mean I have to feel the beauty, but it's an indication for me to acknowledge the beauty.

Gratitude for Life

It has been very important for me to engage in a way of living with gratitude, which is just the simple acknowledgment of something that is precious to me. When I don't acknowledge what is valuable to me, I recognize that perhaps I am taking for granted the fact that I live in a home, I have shelter, I have food, I live with quiet, I live with a partner who is supportive of me, and we have a quality of relationship that is nurturing. I have these animal friends of mine, furry creatures that walk around the house and sometimes do things that are annoying and sometimes do things that are delightful. I can enjoy going outside even if it's raining and grey. There is this existence that I move through in awareness, breathe, and feel my aliveness.

When I engage in this practice of gratitude, I notice it is unending. There is a never-ending recognition and appreciation for so much of life. I get to the place where it is all precious to me. This may be difficult to understand, but even the pain is precious, even the difficulty is precious. When I am awake and I emerge into this space of gratitude, suddenly everything is vibrant; everything is alive. Everything, even pain, is alive. I've touched these moments, and they are exhilarating because they take me beyond my conditioned mind, which is constantly evaluating what is good and what is bad, what is right and what is wrong. The practice of living with an open heart invites gratitude, it even welcomes the experience we call pain.

So, as I take in all of life, moment by moment, what awakens in me? What arises in me? This inquiry practice draws my attention to feel fully what is stirring in me. It draws me to look at and to notice the thoughts and stories that are going through my mind. Can I acknowledge them and see that they are products of my mind in reaction rather than a reflection of some projected reality that is true?

My heart is my guide in life. What I value and what I care about are the guidelines that help me to connect to those qualities that are inherent in my life. I am responsible for staying in tune with what I am needing and what I am valuing. I want to speak and act from that place of awareness rather than to speak and act from a place in which I am not connected to my heart or in harmony with what I care about and value.

PRACTICE: Touching the Beauty in Grief and Gratitude

Mourning

In an undefended experience of grief or mourning, there is a loss, an unfulfilled need or value, and the inner experience linked to that longing. What accompanies grief and mourning are deep feelings of sadness, disheartenment, or similar vulnerable feelings that are felt as a sweet pain.

The invitation in this practice is to take time to notice and allow to unfold what is underneath or inside the pain. When we touch into the energy of the unfulfilled need, there's a preciousness to it. There's a beauty in this energy. We want to take our time to stay with the beauty of our need and to feel it fully.

If you are doing this practice alone, you might want to record the questions first and then play your recording, pausing to receive and then respond to each one. You may want to use a journal to note your responses to the questions.

If you are processing with another person, your partner can ask the questions and then wait as a silent witness while you share your responses out loud to each question.

Don't rush through this practice. Wherever it says, "…pause…," this is an invitation to take the time you need to connect with each question so you can fully receive it. Connect to what's alive and then share (perhaps write) what arises.

Let's begin:

I invite you to bring your attention to your body and to your breath. Relax and breathe.

…pause…

Now, name something in the outer world—an event or something that someone did or said—that was not in harmony with what you value or need.

…pause…

Name what you are feeling emotionally, your body energy, and the value or need that was not fulfilled. Name what is precious to you.

…pause…

What are the thoughts you have about this experience, what is the story?

…pause…

Feel whatever pain, disheartenment, or sadness that resonates in this experience.

…pause…

Feel and sense inside of this feeling of pain; what are you longing for? Allow any sadness or mourning that arises. Invite it. Listen to it.

…pause…

What is precious in you?

…pause…

Enter into the full embodiment of the beauty of your need and dwell in the fullness of what is precious in you and absent in your experience.

Gratitude

When we experience gratitude, we feel thankful for something. When we celebrate life (whether in gratitude or mourning), there is an inner resonance we feel with our needs or values. Connecting with the qualities of our needs, we can dwell in their beauty and fullness.

Again, bring your attention to your body and to your breath. Relax and breathe.

—

…pause…

Now, name something in the outer world that you are grateful for (an event, something someone did, or something you observed).

…pause…

Name what you are feeling emotionally, how you are experiencing your body energy, and the value or need that was fulfilled—what is precious to you.

…pause…

Feel and experience the precious longing or qualities of the need that is awakened in you. Feel it, dwell in it. Name what is precious *in you*.

…pause…

Encompass and hold both the outer stimulus and inner experience together.

…pause…

Wherever you finish in this process, end by relaxing into the center of your being, breathing, and feeling.

Share with your partner or journal your gratitude experience.

There is a difference between experiencing the deficiency of needs and mourning the beauty of an unmet need. When I experience deficiency, there is always thinking involved. When mourning the beauty of an unmet need, my awareness is on my heart, and I feel the natural pain that always touches something held with beauty and honored. Mourning always includes a celebration, which is a form of gratitude. Celebration and mourning are both ways of acknowledging our aliveness and our relationship to the life flow.

Chapter 7

Think about the difference this makes in a relationship: "I don't want your love. I want the same love you want. I don't want your love. I want what you want, and we can find It together and share our deepening experience of It. I thought it was your love I wanted, and it hurt so much when you couldn't give it. I even made a bargain that if I gave it to you, I could expect it back. I thought you agreed to this bargain. I thought you were part of the deal.

I lived in fear that your love would disappear. I moved so deeply into the veil. Now I hear within me the whispering of something else. I feel the possibility of a Love that has nothing to do with you—an infinite resource that is always there. This Love is not affected by any condition, nor

does it change in the stream of time. It is the same Love whether my body is strong or weak, whether I am rich and bountiful in material things or whether I am poor. It is not affected by things of this world. This is the Love that brings release. This is the Love that dissolves chains. This is the Love that brings peace. This is the only Love I want. It releases you, my friend, from all our contracts."
~ Stephen Schwartz[14]

Many words are used to express the Divine: God and Spirit are among them. We can experience the reality of the Divine in many ways. When I bring a loving attention to life (to my inner life or to you), that is the Divine manifesting. When there is kindness, that is the Divine. When there are acceptance and love, the Divine is manifesting. In my experience, the Divine goes beyond religion. Although we can use religious approaches to help us connect to the Divine, I don't think the Divine has any kind of religious affiliation.

The central part of this work of Living Compassion can be seen as arriving more fully in life itself. When I arrive in life more fully, then what is here for me is a deeper, more conscious experiencing of life, of attuning to it, and feeling the resonance and dissonance with my core values. When I arrive in life more fully, I am living the full life energy in my joy and from the fullness of life energy that is in my pain.

The other part of this work is that when I am attuned to life and there is another person present with me and for me, this magical, sacred space is created. One human being and another human being are holding each other in a shared space where we can welcome our own and each other's experience without judgment, without reservation.

Communion

The specificity of language that the Nonviolent Communication process teaches can be a conduit for the full flowing of life energy and the transformation of whatever obstructs it. NVC helps me bring my inner world into the relational world. For me, the most important aspect of NVC is the concept of universal human needs. It is this concept that links us to our essence. This way of approaching our authenticity through our needs can support us in giving meaning to the way we are with ourselves and the intentionality with which we approach our relationships.

When we get to the heart of who we are as human beings, we all yearn for a simple, tender way of being with one another. The beauty of this work of Living Compassion is that it brings me to this place where I experience a profound recognition that we are all the same at the deepest human level. There is a universality of the flow of life within, of how we connect with the world, and of how we encounter the obstacles to the life force. I want to connect to life as it flows through me so that I can connect to life as it flows through you. It is the same life that is flowing through both of us.

When we are communicating with each other, what we communicate is our internal realities. When someone is speaking, they are speaking their heart: the qualities, the care, and the pain of whatever is in their heart. It's not that the content and form of what we say don't matter, only that they are indicators of these realities. There is fullness and a beauty in this reality. We can ask ourselves, "Are we listening to this person share what's truly in them? What is their heart really communicating?" This is like a meditation practice where we focus our attention on the essential living energy in ourselves, and in the other person.

Communion is another word for an intimate connection we can experience together as a practice and as a way of living. For communion to occur, it is necessary to create an open space within myself in relation to the other person. In this open space, in the embodied awareness that my needs matter, I receive the other in their needs and mattering, and in this space, we matter together. The life in me and the life in you come from the same source, which is Divine life energy.

The quality, nature, and shape of our lives is entirely dependent on how we meet the life force within and between us. How we choose to meet the life force can open us to the mystery within it. I always want to remember that the essence of any expression, no matter how hard it is to hear, is actually life itself. I want to remember that every expression is life calling for life. When I can experience this not as a mental concept, but in a fully felt, bodily-relaxed stance, this is the living essence of nonviolence, of real compassion.

One way to describe this experience is that we are transforming an "I-it" to an "I-thou" relationship in which we have an unmediated, direct experience of the other rather than through our judgments and projections. In the I-thou relationship, a concept developed by Martin Buber[14], we discover that we have the same basic life energy flowing through us, the same qualities that give us meaning. We all want to be seen, we all value support, and we all thrive when there is honesty and authenticity. Something happens to us as human beings, something comes alive when these qualities are active in our relationships.

When I experience a certain quality of connection with someone—and there is a sense of deep love that is alive in me and in the other person—the words, "You met my need for love," no longer expresses the depth of my experience. When I have this quality of connection, it is not that you have met my needs for acceptance or for compassion; it is more that through this quality of connection, our relationship has become a conduit for these Divine energies. We enter into the energy of love. When we align ourselves with the consciousness and language which supports the energy of love, we move from awareness of separation to awareness of connection.

Although our communication exchange doesn't connect us per se, language helps us remove the obstacles of separation so we can experience the already existing unity. We call this "connection" in NVC. Living this integration and embodiment of the "I" and "we," there's a longing and a way of tapping into and communicating our wholeness so that we can meet another human being in the relational space in our wholeness. This is embodying the qualities of our being in relationship. We experience an "I-thou" relationship. It is the communion of differentiated unity in the "you" and the "me."

The Divine in Relationship

One of the beauties of Nonviolent Communication is that it integrates the eastern, mystical tradition and western psychological, interpersonal communication. This integration allows us this spiritual orientation for approaching human needs.

Many years ago, when I entered my adult life, I immediately began a spiritual and life quest that took the forms of spiritual practice and the study of psychology and communication. My quest ever since has been the integration of these two. Each of these approaches has its richness, but they are incomplete unless I'm integrating them. I've found a necessary consciousness available in the spiritual and mystical traditions. And yet, unless I can live this consciousness in my relationships using language in the space of mutuality, then unity consciousness isn't necessarily helpful to me, particularly when there's disconnection.

Connected with the divine energy within, I want to bring this energy to my relationships. I'm conscious that other people have their own agency. I don't have choice over what they experience, but I can influence them. I can bring an energy, a presence, and an understanding to our relationship and to the degree that I do this, I am living the Divine. It is not an abstraction that is only available to me in special cases, I can bring it into all my relationships. This, for me, is the essence of life. It is the beauty of one human being with another human being, creating the space between us. This is where all the magic happens. This is where the sacred resides.

The Dyad Meditation Process

The Dyad Meditation Process[16] has been one of the most powerful tools for spiritual growth and healing in relationship in my entire life. The Enlightenment Technique[17] on which it is based was the very first practice I learned when I was nineteen or twenty years old. This process creates an unconventional intimacy in which two human beings can meet in vulnerability and with open hearts.

A Dyad is a pair—two people who are sitting and facing each other, attending to one another, taking turns every five minutes either to share or witness. Through the forty-minute process, a quality of depth develops in connection, presence, and awareness.

There are two roles in the Dyad Meditation Process. The first role is the witness. The witness asks a question and then stays completely silent for the entire process, offering soft but constantly available eye contact, if possible. At the end of each five minutes, the witness says, "Thank you."

The second role is the sharing person. This person brings their awareness to their inner life and then shares what arises in their experience as they receive each question from the witness.

This practice is an invitation to show up just as we are with one another as open-hearted human beings, in an undefended intimacy. This is a spiritual practice without dogma; it is a practice of simple presence with the beauty of the human heart. It creates a place where we meet each other in spiritual companionship.

The Dyad Meditation Process is a simple way to help remove the veil that obscures the consciousness of the heart. In this process, we are reminded of this sacred space where two hearts meet, and the Divine emerges. Life is waiting for us to come together and meet in this space of presence where we are already undivided.

Healing in Relationship

What has become increasingly important to me is to explore more deeply and to share with others this space where we meet in authenticity and mutuality. This space can be a profoundly healing one. There can be something deeply sacred in witnessing and being witnessed. In this relational space, I reach outside of myself and vulnerably share and vulnerably receive. As I receive the other, I suspend my reality for a moment and take in their reality; I take in the world as if I am receiving them the way that they experience themselves.

If, while connecting with another person, such as during the Dyad Meditation Process, a longing arises that is related to some deep relational wounding—for example, if that wounding is around trust—it can be challenging to connect with the longing for trust because the trauma carries so much pain of trust not being fulfilled. If you are not able to access the fullness of trust, then this is an indication that whatever arises is there to be embraced with acceptance and compassion. I have found that the sacred process of witnessing in mutuality is an important part of a spiritual practice and it is important for healing. Something that became evident to me a long time ago is that relational wounds can only be healed in relationship.

The Importance of Support

I think it's an incredibly important aspect of this work to acknowledge that what we are doing is not an easy practice for most of us. This work needs support. It can be either inner support or external support. If I don't have the capacity to offer myself internal support, then I want to remember the possibility of receiving external support in the form of a loving presence—someone willing to accompany me without judging me—who can create a space of kindness and can welcome into it whatever I am experiencing. The pain I am holding within myself only yields into a space of kindness. That space of kindness is essential for development and healing.

PRACTICE: Compassion and Authenticity

This practice has more value than just as an exercise; it is a meditation. It is an invitation to dwell in the energies of compassion and authenticity (or whatever needs you choose). This practice cultivates the embodiment of these energies of your aliveness and keeps you centered on what really matters to you.

You might want to record the self-exploration portion of this meditation first and then play your recording. Remember to move slowly through the practice. Note that the "...pause..." is an invitation to give yourself time to notice and connect to what arises in you. If you cannot connect with the fullness of the need, then the invitation is to bring compassion to those parts of you that are in resistance. You can journal your experience at the end.

Self-Exploration: Compassion

Let's begin by bringing your attention to your body and to your breath. Relax and breathe.

...pause...

I invite you to explore the quality of compassion; how compassion lives in you. Begin by accessing a memory, remembering as vividly as you can a time when you experienced compassion...when you were feeling this energy of compassion.

...pause...

Connect to what compassion feels like, how it feels to live in the energy of compassion. Notice its felt qualities...let yourself embody compassion or bring compassion to any resistance.

Sense how living in the energy of compassion feels in your body.

...pause...

Allow yourself to sink into this feeling, into its energy. Allow whatever arises to be there.

...pause...

Dwell in the experience. Write it down. Take whatever time you would like for this.

Self-Exploration: Authenticity

Now do the same process you followed with the quality of compassion but this time, explore the quality of authenticity (or any other need).

Explore whatever authenticity is for you in relationship.

Let's begin by bringing your attention to your body and to your breath. Relax and breathe.

...pause...

Remember a time when you experienced authenticity in a relationship. Bring the memory into your mind as vividly as you can and then focus your awareness on your present moment feelings and body sensations.

...pause...

Allow yourself to relax into whatever you are feeling. Dwell in the energy of authenticity or bring compassion to any resistance. Allow whatever arises to be there.

...pause...

Write it down. Take as much time as you would like for this.

Exploration in Dyad: Compassion

When you do the exercise with a partner, each person does the same process of exploring the need as when processing alone. Use a set amount of time; three to five minutes works well. While you speak, your partner witnesses, listening silently.

Begin by exploring the quality of compassion as you did in the self-exploration practice. Allow whatever arises to come up in your experience. Then, dwell in the energies of compassion or bring compassion to any resistance.

…pause…

Share aloud with your partner whatever emerges in you, within the agreed-upon time.

Next, exchange roles and receive your partner's exploration.

After both of you have had the opportunity to explore the quality of compassion and to share, you may want to pause and transition to exploring authenticity with your partner.

Exploration in Dyad: Authenticity

Begin by exploring the quality of authenticity as you did in the self-exploration practice. Allow whatever arises to come up in your experience.

...pause...

Dwell in the energies of authenticity or bring compassion to any resistance.

...pause...

Share aloud with your partner whatever emerges in you within the agreed-upon time.

Then, exchange roles and receive your partner's exploration.

We are in relationship all the time whether we are in direct relationship with another person or not. We exist as "unity-in-relationship" with everything. With awareness of the wholeness of the world comes the awareness that my needs and your needs matter. Mutuality flowers from this awareness.

Living Compassion

All of spirituality is my relationship to life energy as it is offered to me and through me, to the totality of life. This happens through all the forms of relationship and through other people. Spirituality is the life in me and the life in you.

A spiritual life practice can be seen as addressing our relationship with this life force within and outside of us. It will sweep us into living experiences. The direction and quality of how we allow the life force to sweep us and to flow through us is dependent upon our awareness and choice.

We are spiritual beings. This spiritual dimension is accessible in everyday life, both internally and in relationship. By bringing this dimension of ourselves into relationship, our beings and our lives are both enriched.

The relationship space where we invite each other into this mutual experience is one in which I show up and you show up in our vulnerable authenticity. This is the field of Rumi's poem:

Out beyond ideas of
wrongdoing and rightdoing,
there is a field. I'll meet you there.
When the soul lies down in that grass,
the world is too full to talk about.
Ideas, language, even the phrase 'each other'
doesn't make any sense.
~ Jelaluddin Rumi[18]

This is an actual space where we live with one another. And, for me, it is the heart of the Nonviolent Communication process. This is where spirituality lives.

Afterword

Vision and Dream for Living Compassion

In the many years that I have shared the work of Living Compassion, I have been blessed and inspired by the love and courage I have experienced and witnessed with thousands of people. In March 2020, I received a message from one of them, my dear friend, Andie Nagel[19], in which she described a dream she'd had for Living Compassion.

As I received Andie's message, I was struck by the synchronicity of her dream, as the same dream has lived in me for many years. My strong sense of how dreams radiate from the human heart into life is that they are a creative force that comes from the very essence of Life. As I surrender to the energy of love, there is a living intelligence that flows and guides me. As I surrender to the force of life, it brings me more alive. It is as if the energy is a great attractor.

In my vision, I see people all over the world sharing and living compassion. In this vision, we are living in "islands of aliveness and compassion," responding to the deeper dream that lives in the field of life, from our deepest longings, to embody love and compassion. In my experience, one of the central features of compassion is community. We come together with a shared purpose to create spaces in which all of the parts of us—our pain, trauma, joys, and love—are welcome. In this welcoming space, we invoke the Presence of Life, we surrender our fear, and we allow the love that is at the heart of all human experience to emerge.

With love and community,

Robert

Endnotes

[1] Robert Gonzales, *Reflections on Living Compassion: Awakening Our Passion and Living in Compassion* (2015)

[2] Stephen Schwartz, *The Compassionate Presence* (1988)

[3] Matt Licata, posted on his Facebook page, August 18, 2015

[4] Stephen Schwartz, *The Compassionate Presence* (1988)

[5] Stephen Schwartz, *The Compassionate Presence* (1988)

[6] Stephen Schwartz, *The Compassionate Presence* (1988)

[7] Sarah McLean, *The Power of Attention* (2017)

[8] Lawrence Heller and Aline La Pierre, *Healing Developmental Trauma: How Early Trauma Affects Self-Regulation, Self-Image, and the Capacity for Relationship* (2012)

[9] Steven Harrison, *What's Next After Now?: Post-Spirituality and the Creative Life* (2005)

[10] Alan Watts, *The Wisdom of Insecurity: A Message for an Age of Anxiety* (1951)

[11] Henry Wadsworth Longfellow, excerpted from "The Poet's Tale; The Birds of Killingworth", *Tales of a Wayside Inn* (1863)

[12] John Green, *Looking for Alaska* (2006)

[13] John Welwood, *Love and Awakening* (1997)

[14] Stephen Schwartz, *The Compassionate Presence* (1988)

[15] Martin Buber, *I and Thou* (1923)

[16] Global Dyad Meditation Program, www.globaldyadmeditation.org

[17] Charles Berner, *Enlightenment and the Enlightenment Intensive, 5 Essays* (2013)

[18] Jelaluddin Rumi, excerpted from "A Great Wagon", Rumi: *Selected Poems* (translation by Coleman Barks), (2004)

[19] Andie Nagel, formerly Andie Steidl

[20] Robert Gonzales, *Reflections on Living Compassion: Awakening Our Passion and Living in Compassion* (2015)

About the Author

Robert Gonzales' work of Living Compassion has emerged from more than 30 years of teaching Nonviolent Communication (NVC) and a lifetime of inquiry into the intersection between spirituality and human communication. His influences included Dr. Marshall Rosenberg (founder of Nonviolent Communication),

Stephen Schwartz (creator of Compassionate Self-Care), and other spiritual teachers.

Robert received a PhD in Clinical Psychology in 1989, and he was a practicing therapist for many years. He met Marshall Rosenberg in 1985 and began teaching NVC in 1986. Robert contributed to the work of the Center for Nonviolent Communication (CNVC) as a Certified Trainer, a Certification Assessor, and as Board President. He also co-founded the NVC Training Institute.

Robert founded the Center for Living Compassion in 2000 as a result of what he referred to as "a calling" to focus on, grow, and share his work of Living Compassion. Robert's first book, *Reflections on Living Compassion: Awakening Our Passion and Living in Compassion*[20], was published in 2015.

In December 2020, Robert articulated his "Vision and Dream" for expanding Living Compassion, and he invited others to join him in bringing this to life. Robert intended this Vision and Dream to be a guide for bringing the Living Compassion community into a global network of connection and mutual support to live and expand compassion throughout the world. More about Robert's Vision and Dream is in the Afterword.

Robert's teachings and practices have and continue to help thousands of people worldwide to find healing and freedom from suffering, previously unavailable to them. Robert Gonzales left his body near midnight on November 19, 2021.

ABOUT THE PUBLICATION TEAM

Filipa Hope (www.filipahope.com) is a certified NVC trainer who assisted Robert Gonzales in the program on which this book is based, as well as his other online offerings. In addition to attending Robert's LIFE Program in the United States and New Zealand, she assisted at his last LIFE Program in the United States and at other retreats. Filipa was part of the team that supported the publication of Robert's book, Reflections on Living Compassion: Awakening Our Passion and Living in Compassion, in 2015. She is the Content Creator for the NVC mobile app NVConnect. Filipa lives in Hawke's Bay, New Zealand.

Simone Anliker (www.simoneanliker.com) is a certified NVC trainer, a certified Havening

Techniques® practitioner and trainer, and a certified NARM Trauma Master Practitioner. In addition to assisting Robert in his Euro-LIFE Program (2010-2014) and his Australia-New Zealand LIFE Program (2014-2015), Simone co-led several international retreats with Robert. She was part of the team that supported the publication of Robert's book, Reflections on Living Compassion: Awakening Our Passion and Living in Compassion, in 2015 and is the author of her own book, The Power of Dyad Meditation: A New Way of Meditating in Times of Loneliness and Social Stress, published in 2020. She lives in Flüeli-Ranft, Switzerland.

Lynd Morris was a member of the first LIFE Program Robert Gonzales offered in 2006. She assisted him in numerous NVC trainings across the United States and was an original member of the team that supported Robert in developing his work of Living Compassion. Lynd became a CNVC-certified trainer in 2009 and in addition to developing her own Welcoming LIFE Program, she co-led Living Compassion retreats with Robert, Simone, and others in 2013 and 2014. A professional writer for nearly 40 years, Lynd lives outside Washington DC, United States.

In Gratitude

We are deeply grateful to our friends and colleagues who contributed to seeing this book through to publication. We could not have moved as quickly and effectively without the care and contributions of Bett Farber, Jeff Brown, Mary Scholl, Andie Nagel, Herman Veluwenkamp, Zandra Hughes, Manfred Friedrich, Richard Broadbent, and many others whose support has made this book a reality. We are especially grateful for the loving support and blessings of Robert's wife, Ruth Joy.

The proceeds of this book go, with love, to Ruth.

Made in United States
North Haven, CT
15 July 2024

54833826R00134